MW01249016

Collaborative Teaching in the Middle Grades

Collaborative Teaching in the Middle Grades

Inquiry Science

Helaine Becker

A Member of the Greenwood Publishing Group

Westport, Connecticut ● London

British Library Cataloguing in Publication Data is available.

Copyright © 2005 by Libraries Unlimited

All rights reserved. No portion of this book may be
reproduced, by any process or technique, without the
express written consent of the publisher.

ISBN: 1-59158-191-5

First published in 2005

Libraries Unlimited, 88 Post Road West, Westport, CT 06881
A Member of the Greenwood Publishing Group, Inc.
www.lu.com

Printed in the United States of America

The paper used in this book complies with the
Permanent Paper Standard issued by the National
Information Standards Organization (Z39.48–1984).

10 9 8 7 6 5 4 3 2 1

The author and publisher gratefully acknowledge permission for use of the following material:

Excerpts from *Benchmarks for Scientific Literacy: Project 2061* by American Association for the Advancement
of Science, copyright © 1993 by the American Association for the Advancement of Science. Used by permission
of Oxford University Press, Inc.

Excerpts from the Information Standards for Student Learning from *Information Power: Building Partnerships
for Learning* prepared by the American Association of School Librarians and the Association for Educational
Communications and Technology. Copyright © 1998. Used by permission of the American Library Association.

For my sister,
Jacqueline Maguire,
who teaches special needs children with love,
understanding, and dedication.

"A teacher affects eternity; he can never tell where his influence stops."
—Henry Adams

Contents

Introduction

Information Science in a Postmodern World

In the last decade, school library and media services have completely transformed. At the heart of this metamorphosis is *Information Power: Building Partnerships for Learning,* a set of professional guidelines developed by the American Association of School Librarians (AASL) and the Association for Educational Communications and Technology (AECT) and published in 1998. *Information Power* was partially a response to a crisis in information science delivery. In a time of budget tightening and competing educational agendas, school library and media programs were more and more frequently being seen as a frill. The library was viewed as a support to the all-important three Rs, but not important in and of itself. The document sought to reclaim the library's central role in education by highlighting the principles and practices of quality information literacy programs.

Information Power was also a call to action. It provided practicing information science specialists with an outline for how to strengthen their school library and media programs. It presented clearly delineated standards of achievement and benchmarks for assessing the success of a school library and media program. It also demonstrated how information literacy could and should be at the foundation of every school's mission statement. *Information Power* provided the theoretical basics for guiding students through the data deluge of the postmodern world.

Implementing *Information Power*

Information Power mandated information literacy programs that were "designed around active, authentic learning." It also urged information science professionals to update their programs to ensure that

- Learning activities are integrated into the curriculum;

- Emphasis is placed on strategies that develop effective cognitive strategies for "selecting, retrieving, analyzing, evaluating, synthesizing, creating, and communicating information in all formats and in all content areas of the curriculum"; and

- Programs offer leadership, collaboration, and assistance to teachers in other disciplines in applying information science skills.

Collaborative Teaching

Information Power provided guidelines and inspiration for creating a model program. But it did not offer specific lessons or activities to apply them. How can school library professionals like you go the next step? How can you create authentic learning across the curriculum, in your own library media center?

The answer is found in collaboration with others. By joining forces with like-minded professionals in other curriculum areas, you can teach superior cross-curricular lessons that provide students with curricular related, authentic learning experiences *and* teach critical information literacy skills. You can give students the opportunity to apply a wealth of information literacy skills to coursework in another discipline, thereby underscoring their value and utility. You can reinforce the importance of problem solving and critical thinking skills, learned from your program, in other disciplines. And you can enrich your own program by drawing on the skills and talents of professionals with expertise in different subject areas.

Collaborating with a Science Specialist

A collaboration with a science specialist is a natural place to start. Why? Because the goals of the modern science teacher are remarkably in synch with those of the information specialist.

Like library and media professionals, science teachers are guided by an umbrella document that outlines goals to strive for and principles to follow. These goals are outlined in *Benchmarks for Science Literacy*, published by the American Association for the Advancement of Science (AAAS). This document was produced by Project 2061, the AAAS's ongoing effort by both scientists and educators to help transform the US school system. It is the foundation for all current science curricula being used or developed today. It outlines what all students should know or be able to do in science, mathematics, and technology by the end of grades 2, 5, 8, and 12.

Some of Project 2061's intended goals, as specified in *Benchmarks,* are compatible with the goals of *Information Power.* Consider this statement from *Benchmarks'* introduction:

> In a culture increasingly pervaded by science, mathematics and technology, science literacy requires understandings and habits of mind that enable citizens to grasp what those enterprises are up to, to make some sense of how the natural and designed worlds work, to think critically and independently, to recognize and weigh alternative explanations of events and design trade-offs, and to deal sensibly with problems that involve evidence numbers, patterns, logical arguments, and uncertainties.

Drawing on such similar goals, a collaboration with a science specialist will be both practical and highly effective.

About This Book

Collaborative Teaching in the Middle Grades: Inquiry Science was written to help you work "hand in hand" with your school's science specialists. Using this book, you will lead dynamic lessons that fulfill the joint goals for student learning of both the *Information Power* and *Benchmarks for Science Literacy* documents. Each lesson specifically teaches

- Both information literacy skills and general science process skills,

- Both information science content knowledge and general science content knowledge, and

- The critical thinking and problem-solving skills mandated by both professions.

Furthermore, by using the lessons provided by this book, you will fulfill these additional program goals as described in *Information Power.* You will:

- Work with other teachers to plan, conduct, and evaluate learning activities that incorporate information literacy;

- Build and manage collections that support authentic, information-based learning;

- Work with teachers, administrators, and others to plan, design, and implement programs that provide access to the information that is required to meet students' learning goals;

- Encourage a culture of collaboration within the school;

- Develop support for the school library media program throughout the school;

- Exert strong curricular and instructional leadership to promote a curriculum in which information literacy provides a coherent thread across all subjects;

- Take the lead in educational reform by showing connections between information-based learning and the skills students will need in the coming years;

- Take a proactive role in promoting the use of technology by other staff, in determining staff development needs, and by serving as leader in staff development activities;

- Model and promote lifelong learning by pursuing opportunities for staff development and continuing education;

- Act as a technologist to design student experiences that focus on authentic learning, information literacy, and curricular mastery, not simply manipulating machinery; and

- Integrate people, learning, and the tools of technology.

To facilitate the process of collaboration, planning charts—one for each chapter—have been provided to help you and your science partner organize the nitty-gritty of "who does what?"

Using This Book to Teach the General Science Curriculum

Eight comprehensive chapters provide all of the background information, lesson plans, and reproducible materials needed to teach eight complete science units at the middle grade levels. Each unit includes up to 10 lessons that support key science knowledge benchmarks for students in grades 6 to 8. The benchmarks have been selected from across the curriculum and include topics in life science, physical science, earth science, human health, historical perspectives, and ecology.

Because of the broad nature of topics, there should be several units in this book that can readily be integrated into your existing curriculum. To help you identify which will be most applicable to your program, the relevant benchmarks, the science content knowledge covered, and the science skills developed are presented at the beginning of each chapter.

The first part of each unit is usually content-driven and research based. Reproducible worksheets enable students to organize their information and present their work to you for assessment.

The second part of each unit tends to be more analytical in nature. It may include laboratory work and/or a final project that requires an assessment and synthesis of the knowledge gained in part 1.

Using This Book to Teach the Information Literacy Curriculum

The chapters in this book act as comprehensive units to teach the general science curriculum. Within each chapter, however, you will find that each lesson explicitly addresses the concepts and skills that support the information science curriculum. The topics and skills covered are listed at the beginning of each chapter. Refer also to the table below to correlate each unit to the *Information Power* Standards and Indicators.

Skill-based lessons may include learning how to use indexes to find appropriate resource materials, creating a bibliography, writing essays and letters, and creating information products in a variety of media. Students also do activities in which they learn how to use tools such as T-charts, Venn Diagrams, and K-W-L charts to organize information. Reproducible hand-outs that describe each chapter's information science goals are included in each chapter. Reproducible student worksheets for each activity facilitate lesson organization and implementation. Assessment rubrics are provided to help you evaluate student output in a variety of formats: written, oral, dramatic, and graphic.

Although the chapters in this book generally follow the same basic pattern, the lessons that make up each chapter are highly varied in both content and procedure. The variety supports several aspects of the information science curriculum. For example, one lesson may help your students learn how to work independently, (Standards 4, 5, and 6), whereas the next may require students to work in pairs or as part of a larger group (Standard 9). Some lessons demand projects in a written format; others may require a dramatic or PowerPoint presentation (Standards 3 and 5). Oral, dramatic, artistic, written, and scientific forms of expression are represented in different lessons in this book.

Lessons are also varied in that they take advantage of the different resources in your media center and school (Standard 1). One lesson may rely more heavily on print resources, while the next is more Internet-based. Lab work has students create their own data to integrate into their knowledge base. Some projects have students go to each other to gather information. Many projects encourage the use of student journals to record data, store information, and keep track of progress on activities.

Appropriate assessment strategies and tools are provided for each chapter. In each chapter, tools for student self-assessment, project checklists, or rubrics make measuring student performance simple and straightforward.

Last but not least, the lessons and activities in this book will underscore for students the importance of information literacy. They will discover the satisfaction that comes from being able to access information easily, analyze it critically, and apply it appropriately. Now that, of course, is "information power."

References

American Association of School Librarians and the Association for Educational Communications and Technology. *Information Power: Building Partnerships for Learning.* Chicago and London: American Library Association, 1998.

American Association for the Advancement of Science. *Benchmarks for Science Literacy.* New York: Oxford University Press, 1993.

STANDARD (INDICATOR)	CHAPTER #							
	1	**2**	**3**	**4**	**5**	**6**	**7**	**8**
Standard 1: The student who is information literate accesses information efficiently and effectively.	X	X	X	X	X	X	X	X
Indicator 1: Recognizes the need for information	X	X	X	X	X	X	X	X
Indicator 2: Recognizes that accurate and comprehensive information is the basis for intelligent decision making	X	X	X	X	X	X	X	X
Indicator 3: Formulates questions based on information needs	X	X	X	X	X	X	X	X
Indicator 4: Identifies a variety of potential sources of information	X	X	X	X	X	X	X	X
Indicator 5: Develops and uses successful strategies for locating information	X	X	X	X	X	X	X	X
Standard 2: The student who is information literate evaluates information critically and competently.	X	X	X	X	X	X	X	X
Indicator 1: Determines accuracy, relevance, and comprehensiveness	X		X	X	X	X	X	X
Indicator 2: Distinguishes among fact, point of view, and opinion		X	X			X		
Indicator 3: Identifies inaccurate and misleading information				X	X	X	X	X
Indicator 4: Selects information appropriate to the problem or question at hand	X	X	X	X	X	X	X	X
Standard 3: The student who is information literate uses information accurately and creatively.	X	X	X	X	X	X	X	X
Indicator 1: Organizes information for practical application	X	X	X	X	X	X	X	X
Indicator 2: Integrates new information into one's own knowledge	X	X	X	X	X	X	X	X
Indicator 3: Applies information in critical thinking and problem solving	X	X	X	X	X	X	X	X
Indicator 4: Produces and communicates information and ideas in appropriate formats	X	X	X	X	X	X	X	X

STANDARD (INDICATOR)   CHAPTER

	1	2	3	4	5	6	7	8
Standard 4: The student who is an independent learner is information literate and pursues information related to personal interests.				X				
Indicator 1: Seeks information related to various dimensions of personal well-being, such as career interests, community involvement, health matters, and recreational pursuits				X				
Indicator 2: Designs, develops, and evaluates information products and solutions related to personal interests				X				
Standard 5: The student who is an independent learner is information literate and appreciates literature and other creative expressions of information.	X		X		X	X	X	
Indicator 1: Is a competent and self-motivated reader								
Indicator 2: Derives meaning from information presented creatively in a variety of formats			X					
Indicator 3: Develops creative products in a variety of formats	X		X		X	X	X	
Standard 6: The student who is an independent learner is information literate and strives for excellence in information seeking and knowledge generation.	X			X	X			X
Indicator 1: Assesses the quality of process and products of information seeking	X			X	X			
Indicator 2: Devises strategies for revising, improving, and updating self-generated knowledge	X			X				X
Standard 7: The student who contributes positively to the learning community and to society is information literate and recognizes the importance of information to a democratic society.	X	X	X	X	X	X	X	X
Indicator 1: Seeks information from diverse sources, contexts, disciplines, and cultures	X	X	X	X	X	X	X	X
Indicator 2: Respects the principle of equitable access to information								

STANDARD (INDICATOR)	CHAPTER #							
	1	**2**	**3**	**4**	**5**	**6**	**7**	**8**
Standard 8: The student who contributes positively to the learning community and to society is information literate and practices ethical behavior in regard to information and information technology.	X	X	X	X	X	X	X	X
Indicator 1: Respects the principles of intellectual freedom								
Indicator 2: Respects intellectual property rights	X	X	X	X	X	X	X	X
Indicator 3: Uses information technology responsibly	X	X	X	X	X	X	X	X
Standard 9: The student who contributes positively to the learning community and to society is information literate and participates effectively in groups to pursue and generate information.	X	X		X	X	X	X	
Indicator 1: Shares knowledge and information with others	X	X				X	X	
Indicator 2: Respects others' ideas and backgrounds and acknowledges their contributions	X					X	X	
Indicator 3: Collaborates with others, both in person and through technologies, to identify information problems and to seek their solutions	X	X			X	X	X	
Indicator 4: Collaborates with others, both in person and through technologies, to design, develop, and evaluate information products and solutions	X	X		X	X	X	X	

Alike or Different?:
Classification of Organisms

Object of This Lesson

In this unit, students use library resources and a variety of research tools to explore plant and animal taxonomy. They will learn, through a study of the ideas of Linneaus, how a formal system of classification was developed.

Students will then apply what they have learned to identify various features of living creatures and assign them to an appropriate classification according to standard taxonomic systems.

This unit will support the following American Association for the Advancement of Science Benchmarks (p. 104):

- To understand that classification systems are human-made and can vary with time.

- To recognize that the growth of knowledge about various organisms required changes in taxonomic systems.

- To become familiar with some of the great scientific personages (Linnaeus) who developed classification systems and, by doing so, furthered scientific knowledge.

- To identify structures within various living creatures.

- To classify creatures according to standard taxonomic systems.

Science Content Knowledge and Skills

Students will

- Describe orally and in writing why classification is useful in understanding organisms,

- Describe orally and in writing how and when Linnaeus developed his ideas,

- Explain why Linneaus's system is so useful to modern scientists,

- Describe at least three different ways organisms can be classified,

- Discuss homologous and non-homologous adaptations and how they each arise,

- Identify an organism using its scientific name and list its nearest relatives, and

- Describe the features of an organism that demonstrate its family relationships with other species in its class.

Information Literacy Knowledge and Skills

Students will

- Use a variety of different index types to locate material,

- Describe how they found and chose their resources,

- Evaluate the appropriateness of the research material,

- Identify three different types of media used to find the information required,

- Organize information for practical application,

- Integrate and apply new information,

- Choose the appropriate format for presenting information and explain the choice,

- Apply appropriate strategies for updating and improving work,

- Integrate knowledge and information with that of others in the group,

- Help to organize and integrate the contributions of all the members of the group into information products,

- Participate actively in discussions with others to devise solutions to information problems that integrate group members' information and ideas, and

- Work with others to create and evaluate complex information products that communicate complex information and ideas.

Lesson Outline

This lesson is designed to be team-taught by a library media specialist and a science specialist. Before you introduce the lesson to students, decide which aspects of the unit will be presented by each member of the team. Decide who will assess student performance on each component of the unit. Use the checklist at the end of this chapter to assist you in organizing these aspects of teaching this unit.

Stimulate interest in the lesson by asking students to describe three animals, for example, a swordfish, an elephant, and a clam. Make a list of characteristics for each animal on the blackboard.

Draw a generic family tree on the blackboard. Explain to students that scientists believe that all living creatures evolved from a single-celled bacterium. As they adapted and changed through the process of natural selection, different traits arose. Draw five branches on the tree to illustrate the five kingdoms: Monera, Protista, Fungi, Plantia, and Animalia. Explain that living things that are most closely related share a larger number of traits. They can be shown closer together on the family tree. Ask students which of the five branches on the family tree contain "twigs" for the elephant, fish, and clam (Animalia).

Ask students which of the three animals—clam, elephant, and swordfish—they think are most closely related. Have students explain their reasoning. Some may say the clam and swordfish are more closely related because they live in the ocean or have gills. Others may say, correctly, that the elephant and the fish are more closely related because they have backbones.

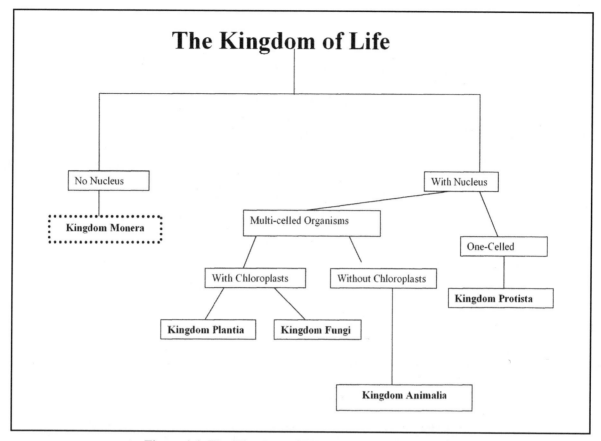

Figure 1.1. The Kingdom of Life. *Source:* **Michael Szasz.**

Explain to students that you will be leading a research project on the subject of taxonomy to help them answer the question definitively. Explain that scientists have been debating classification systems from the earliest days of inquiry. Many different ways of classifying plants and animals exist. Discuss the notion that all classification systems are human-made constructs, and are, in a sense, arbitrary. At the same time, certain types of classification systems have proven to be extremely useful. These are the ones that are employed today.

Explain that the students will be conducting research in the subject by consulting many different types of sources. Ask students where they might find information on this topic. Create a list of possible sources of information on the blackboard.

Point out the list of sources on the blackboard. Ask students how they would find the appropriate materials in each category. Make sure students understand how to use the various indexing tools available in the information center.

Tell students that scientific classification systems are a method for organizing and understanding data. Ask them how they will organize the information they collect for this project. Brainstorm methods and materials to help in the organization and retrieval of data for this project. Discuss common visual tools such as Venn diagrams as tools to show relationships between data or objects. As a way to relate classification systems to everyday life, discuss Web pages and how Web sites are organized into hierarchies.

Ask students if they have any questions about how to proceed with the first step of the project. Review as needed. It may be helpful to list all the steps required for completion of this project on the blackboard. Encourage students to use the checklist of steps to keep track of their work on Student Worksheet 1-A.

Student Worksheet 1-A

Name _____ Date _____

Research Project Checklist 1

Use this checklist to help you organize and track your work on each part of this project.

☐ I have used at least **six** different resources in total. They are:

_____

_____

_____

_____

_____

_____

☐ I have used at least **three** different types of resources (Web page, book, periodical, etc.). These are:

Type of resource—Title _____

Type of resource—Title _____

Type of resource—Title _____

☐ I have used at least **one** primary source. It is: _____

_____

_____

☐ I can create a complete bibliography entry for each of the above sources.

Part 1—Classification of Organisms

Background Information for the Teacher and Library Media Specialist

History of Taxonomy

Taxonomy is probably the oldest science. As an example, consider that people have always classified plants into categories of edibility.

As human society developed, so did our needs for classification. Whether plants were useful for weapons or for clothing, to make shelter or to make medicine forced humans to carefully analyze and group them.

Gradually, our understanding of plants and animals grew. By the time of the ancient Greeks, knowledge about them began to be formalized and recorded. Theophrastos (ca. 300 B.C.) is considered the "grandfather of botany." He wrote more than 200 works, including *Enquiry into Plants* and *The Causes of Plants*. His classifications were based on distinctions between external and internal structures, between flowering and nonflowering plants, and between sexual and asexual reproduction.

The Middle Ages and the Renaissance

During the Middle Ages, very little new work was done in scientific research. One exception was Albertus Magnus (ca. 1250). His classifications recognized the differences between monocots and dicots and between vascular and nonvascular plants.

During the Renaissance, two major technological innovations contributed to the growth of taxonomic science. These were the printing press and navigation. The printing press made books such as herbals popular and accessible. Suddenly, many more people were able to apply scientific knowledge to their own observations of the natural world.

Around the same time, improvements in navigation launched the age of exploration. Explorers brought home specimens of previously unknown species of plants and animals. The number of known plants and animals soared. New systems of classification were needed to handle this increase.

One such system was proposed by Caesalpino. He suggested that classification should be rooted in logic rather than utilitarian concepts (such as medicinal uses). He said that some features are more meaningful than others in classification, for example, the shape of flowers or the number of petals.

It was Carol Linnaeus, however, who made the greatest leaps forward in the science of taxonomy.

Linnaeus

Also known as Carl von Linné, Linnaeus was born on May 23, 1707, at Stenbrohult, in Sweden. He went to the University of Lund in 1727 to study medicine, then transferred to the University of Uppsala, the most prestigious university in Sweden.

Linnaeus spent most of his time at Uppsala studying plants, which were his true love. Despite financial hardship, he mounted a botanical expedition to Lapland in 1731, and another to central Sweden in 1734.

1n 1735, he published the first edition of his classification of living things, the *Systema Naturae*. As more specimens were sent to him from around the world, it evolved from a pamphlet to a multivolume work.

What made Linnaeus's ideas so important was how he grouped species. His contemporaries often used arbitrary criteria to group organisms. For example, they might place all domestic animals or all water animals together. Linnaeus's innovation was to group genera into higher *taxa*. The taxa also were based on shared similarities. Genera were grouped into orders. Orders were grouped into classes, and classes were grouped into kingdoms.

Another of Linnaeus's innovations was in naming species. Before Linnaeus, naming practices varied. After experimenting with several versions, Linnaeus simplified the process dramatically. He designated one Latin name for the genus, and one Latin name for the species. The two names together form a complete *binomial* ("two names") species name. Linnaeus's binomial names quickly became the standard.

Linnaeus's plant taxonomy was based on the number and arrangement of the reproductive organs. He readily admitted that this produced an "artificial classification," not a natural one, and that this was a weakness.

The sexual basis of Linnaeus's plant classification was also controversial in its day. Although it was easy to learn and use, it tended to result in strange classifications that did not seem logical. For example, cacti and pines were classified together because they had numerous male parts. Its emphasis on sex was also considered extremely vulgar.

Further Developments

Another botanist, Michel Adanson, rejected the Linnaean system. Adanson thought that relying on one trait such as reproductive organ shape was too limiting. He thought that assessing many different characteristics at once would lead to the most natural or useful classification. Adansonian taxonomy, also called the phenetic system of Numerical Taxonomy, grew out of these ideas.

A French family called de Jussieu had a different method of classification. They grouped plants by appearance, a so-called natural system. They arranged the plants in the Paris botanical garden in this fashion. Two English botanists, George Bentham and Sir Joseph D. Hooker, also used a "natural" system in the 1800s to lay out Kew Gardens.

It was Charles Darwin's *On the Origin of the Species*, however, that provided the next major leap in taxonomy. New relationships based on evolutionary history—phylogeny—could now be posited and proven. Since Darwin's time, most systems of classification have tried to reflect evolutionary relationships.

Taxonomy Today

When researchers discover an unknown organism, they begin their study by looking for anatomical features that appear to have the same function as those found in other species. The next step is to determine the reason for the similarity. Are both species descended from a common ancestor? If so, then their similarities are called *homologies*. The more homologies two organisms possess, the more likely they are to be closely related.

But not all creatures that share similar organs with similar functions share their ancestry. There can also be non-homologous structural similarities between species. The similarities may have arisen independently in separate evolutionary lines. One example of a non-homologous structural similarity is the vertebrate eye and the eye of the octopus. While they appear similar and share the same function, they arose independently. Superficial similarities can easily fool researchers who do not have a solid understanding of evolutionary history.

Problems in Classifying Organisms

Classifying organisms has the unintentional effect of making the organisms seem, somehow, *fixed.* By fitting organisms into an artificial, static framework, it becomes easy to overlook the changes that are constantly occurring within each organism.

Similarly, it is easy to forget that most species are genetically diverse. Generalities make classification simple. But at the same time, they tend to blur the huge variety that exists even within a species.

Another problem in classifying organisms is deciding which characteristics are the important ones for distinguishing each one from all other types of organisms. It is not always obvious which traits are most significant. Nor will all researchers agree. Comparisons of DNA are now commonly used to settle these differences. If two animals share a large percentage of DNA sequences, they are probably closely related.

DNA, however, is not conclusive in determining if two organisms are members of the same species. Therefore, we must still rely on *morphological* characteristics—appearance—to identify species' differences.

In conclusion, taxonomy is useful as an aid for understanding the structures and relationships of living things. But ultimately, it is only a human construct, one that reflects the biases and ideologies of its makers.

Glossary

- Analogous —similar or comparable in certain aspects

- Cladogram—a branching diagram to illustrate speciation and the relationships between species

- Class—a major category in the classification of living things, ranking above an order and below a division or phylum

- Genus—a major category in the classification of living things, ranking above a species and below a family

- Homologous—corresponding in basic type of structure and deriving from a common primitive organ

- Kingdom—a major category in the classification of living things, ranking above a division or phylum

- Order—a major category in the classification of living things, ranking above a family and below a class

- Phylogeny—the evolutionary lines of descent of any plant or animal species

- Species—a naturally existing population of similar organisms that interbreed only among themselves

- Taxonomy—the system of classification whereby plants and animals are arranged into natural, related groups based on common factors

Information for the Student:
Classification of Organisms

In this unit, you will explore how organisms have been classed in different ways as a means to understand them. You will also meet a giant in the field of science, Linnaeus, who created the basic classification system that scientists use today.

To succeed in this activity, you will need to do research using a variety of media and information sources. You will then need to apply what you have learned to identify and classify a mystery organism. As you perform your research, keep in mind the following questions:

- Where are the best places to find the information I need? What types of materials will be the most useful?

- Is the source for my information reliable and accurate? Who is providing the information?

- Is the information relevant? How does this source help me answer the questions I am being asked or solve the problem being posed?

- How can I organize the information I find to make effective use of it when I need it?

At the end of this unit, you will prepare a cladogram (a family "tree") that shows your mystery animal and its nearest relatives.

Keep all of your work on this project—notes, worksheets, and reference information— together in a file folder or binder.

Student Worksheet 1-1

Name _____ **Date** _____

The Language of Classification

Use a dictionary to find these terms. Write the definitions on this worksheet.

- Analogous _____

  _____

- Cladogram _____

  _____

- Class _____

  _____

- Genus _____

  _____

- Homologous _____

  _____

- Kingdom _____

  _____

- Order _____

  _____

- Phylogeny _____

  _____

- Species _____

  _____

- Taxonomy _____

  _____

Student Worksheet 1-2

Name _____ Date _____

Linnaeus and the Development of Taxonomic Systems

Linnaeus was a Swedish scientist who lived in the 18th century. He created a system of taxonomy that is still used today. It is one of the most important developments in the history of science.

Use at least **four** different sources to find out about Linnaeus's life and work. Choose at least **three** different types of sources, such as reference books, periodicals, Web sites, or encyclopedias.

Which resource will you check first? _____

    Why? _____

_____

Which resource will you check next? _____

    Why? _____

_____

Then answer the following questions:

- What was Carol Linnaeus's profession? _____

_____

- What was the name of the book Linnaeus published in 1735? _____

_____

- Describe, in your own words, Linnaeus's taxonomic system. _____

_____

- Linnaeus was a very influential professor. What did many of his students do that advanced scientific knowledge? _____

_____

- What was one drawback of the Linnean system? _____

_____

Student Worksheet 1-3

Name _____ **Date** _____

Other Systems of Taxonomy

Linnaeus was not the first or the last person to propose a system of classification for living things. Many other people had ideas on this subject. Use at least **four** different sources to find out more about other systems of classification that have been used in different times and places.

Use Research Project Checklist 1 (Student Worksheet 1-A) to help organize your work. List the types of resources you will need. Check them off as you find and read them. Write down the name of each source and other details for future reference and to create a bibliography.

- What did Aristotle have to say about plant or animal classification?

  _____

- What did Albertus Magnus have to say about plant or animal classification?

  _____

- What two scientific advances in the Renaissance period spurred the development of new classification systems?

  _____

- How did Charles Darwin's theories of natural selection affect the science of taxonomy?

  _____

- List three different ways you might logically classify animals. On the back of this sheet, use Venn diagrams to illustrate your groupings.

  _____

  _____

  _____

  _____

Student Worksheet 1-4

Name _____ Date _____

Writing a Persuasive Essay

Consider the following statement:

Butterflies and birds are closely related because they both can fly.

Use the back of this sheet to write a short essay explaining why you agree or disagree with this statement. You will use what you have learned while doing your research to support your argument.

Your essay should include three main sections:

- an introductory paragraph,

- at least one body paragraph, and

- a concluding paragraph.

Your *introductory paragraph* will set out the main purpose of your essay. Your purpose will be to either prove or disprove the statement given above.

Write one sentence that describes your main purpose here:

_____

_____

The *body* of your essay will provide the proof that supports your main point. Each item of proof is given its own paragraph. The paragraph should also include details that illustrate the main idea of the paragraph.

List each of the reasons that support your essay's main purpose. Each of these will become the foundation for its own paragraph. The more reasons you list, the stronger and more persuasive your essay will be.

_____

Paragraph 1: _____

Paragraph 2: _____

Paragraph 3: _____

For each of the reasons you have listed above, be prepared to provide facts and other details to illustrate them. Use the space below to jot down your notes. If you cannot think of supportive details, you will have to go back to your original research notes or do additional research.

The *concluding paragraph* of your essay restates your main point. It also sums up the main ideas in each of your body paragraphs.

When you have completed your essay, make sure you proofread your work. Check for spelling and punctuation errors and factual accuracy. Revise your work as necessary.

Assessment for Student Worksheet 1-4

Name _____ **Date** _____

Quality of Content

3   Message is clear to the reader. Content is solid. All facts in each body paragraph support the essay's main idea. Author clearly understands the material.

2   The reader is unsure of the main message of the essay. Content is uneven in quality. Some evidence supports the main idea. Other evidence detracts from the message. Author has a moderate level of understanding of the material.

1   No clear message is presented. Content is weak. Body paragraphs bear little relation to the main idea. Author seems to not have a grasp on the material.

Organization

3   Essay is well organized. All three main components—intro, body, and conclusion—are present. Order of body paragraphs makes sense.

2   Essay is somewhat organized. Some of the main components are present.

1   Essay is not well organized. Paragraphs do not have a coherent order. Material is confusing.

Style

3   Essay is written with excellent style. Sentence structure is clear and elegant. Transitions between ideas are handled smoothly. Scientific terms are used appropriately.

2   Essay is competent. Style is pedestrian but effectively communicates ideas. Transitions are occasionally rocky. Scientific terms are not used or are used uncertainly.

1   Essay is sloppy. Sentences are awkward or incomplete. Transitions between ideas are nonexistent or weak. Language is simplistic.

Mechanics

3   Entire essay is neat and attractive. Grammar, spelling, and punctuation are all used properly.

2   Some parts of the essay are neat and attractive. Grammar, spelling, and punctuation are imperfect or applied inconsistently.

1   The essay is sloppy. The writer seems to have used little care in preparing the essay. Consistent and correct grammar, spelling, and punctuation are noticeably absent.

Part 2—Animal Classification in Practice

Background Information for the Teacher and Library Media Specialist

In part 2 of this unit, students will apply what they have learned about plant and animal classification to the classification of a mystery animal. Students will be separated into groups of five or fewer to collaboratively identify one of six "mystery animals." The mystery animals are each described on a separate handout.

Lesson Outline

Stimulate interest in this portion of the unit by handing out the mystery animal cards (see pages 21–22). Explain to students that they will be using what they have learned about taxonomy to identify a mystery animal. They will then prepare a cladogram for the animal that shows its nearest relatives. Explain that the cladogram will be created in a group. Allow students to choose groups of up to five individuals.

Ask students how they might proceed to find the information about their mystery animals. Brainstorm a list of steps students might take to solve the problem. What reference material did students find in part 1 of this unit that may help them in part 2? Have students share their sources to create a class bibliography.

Review the terms defined on Student Worksheet 1-1, "The Language of Classification."

Ask students if they have any questions about how to proceed with the project. Review as needed. Then hand out the mystery animal worksheets.

Student Worksheet 1-5

Name _____ **Date** _____

Cooperative Project Checklist

Use this checklist to help you organize and track your work on this project.

☐ My partners and I have discussed the description of our mystery animal.

☐ We prepared a list of key features of our mystery animal.

☐ We brainstormed a list of possible classes and genera to which our mystery animal might belong.

☐ We searched for our mystery animal in several places. These are the references we used:

_____

_____

_____

_____

☐ We have found a possible identification for our mystery animal. We think our animal is:

_____

☐ We have prepared a rough draft of a cladogram that shows our mystery animal. Its three nearest relatives are:

_____

☐ We have decided on the format to present our good copy of the cladogram.

☐ We have collected the following materials to prepare our cladogram:

_____

_____

_____

_____

☐ We have decided on a heading or title for our cladogram. It is:

_____

☐ We have completed our cladogram for display in the classroom.

_____

Species Descriptions for the Teacher and Library Media Specialist

Mystery Animal 1—Spotted Hyena—*Crocuta crocuta*

Hyenas are closely related to meerkats, mongoose, civets, fossas, and cats. They are found in Africa, southwestern Asia, and India.

Paleontologists know of at least 69 species from the fossil record. The first hyaenid dates back to between 18 and 17 million years ago. Around 10 million years ago, some species evolved into "running hyenas." They ran down their prey like wolves. Others evolved into forms more like small wolves or jackals. Between 6 and 7 million years ago, some became fairly slow bone-crushers, much like several genera of modern hyenas. Only four species of hyaenids exist today.

Hyenas range in size from 10 to 80 kilograms. They have bushy tails and rounded ears. Some have a mane. Each species has a distinctive coat. The hyena walks on its toes. Its claws are blunt and cannot be retracted.

A distinguishing feature of the hyena is the difference in length between the front and rear limbs. This gives it the perpetual appearance of running uphill.

A group of hyenas is called a clan. Clans are centered around the females, which are both dominant over and larger than the males. Female hyenas generally stay with the clan in which they were born. Males leave the clan when they become sexually mature.

The spotted hyena, *crocutus crocutus*, is sometimes known as the laughing hyena because of the distinctive sounds it makes. Its coat is spotted and varies and changes with age. It has a well-developed, muscular neck and large ears set high on its head.

Spotted hyenas are skilled hunters, quite capable of taking down large prey. They have massive jaws and large bone-crushing teeth. They live in varied terrain and climates, ranging from deserts to mountain, from flat, grassy plains to marshes. They are found in Africa south of the Sahara desert (except for the Congo basin).

Mystery Animal 2—Giant Squid—*Architeuthidae dux*

The *Architeuthidae* are the largest known cephalopods, the largest known mollusks, and probably the largest invertebrates ever to exist in the oceans. Largest specimens attain total lengths up to 18 meters. The heaviest animals weigh about a ton, but most of the time they are 500 kilograms or less.

The giant squid have the largest eyes of any animal in the world. The eyes of the giant squid can be as big as a human's head. They also have two feeding tentacles, each averaging about 10 to 12 meters in length. The tentacles have many suckers on the tips, called clubs. The clubs are narrow and have suckers themselves.

The *Architeuthidae's* fins are relatively small, egg-shaped, and without free anterior lobes. The fins at the rear of the mantle help the squid move by gentle, rhythmic pulses of water pushed out of the mantle cavity throughout the funnel, two very large gills resting inside the mantle cavity. The squid breathe and move quickly by expanding the mantle cavity.

Eight arms with suckers are aligned in two longitudinal rows. At the base of the arms are parrotlike beaks. The nervous system of the squid is very extensive. Squid also have a complex brain. For this reason they are under extensive research.

Only three generally recognized species of *Architeuthidae* exist. The most common species is **A. dux**, which lives in the North Atlantic Ocean, and which is the "mystery animal." The others are **A. martensi**, found in the North Pacific, and **A. sanctipauli**, which lives in the Southern Ocean.

Mystery Animal 3—Nine-Banded Armadillo—*Dasypus novemcinctus*

Armadillos are classified in the phylum Chordata, subphylum Vertebrata, class Mammalia, order Edentata, family Dasypodidae. There are 21 armadillo species, classified in 9 genera. They range from Argentina to Panama and into the southern United States. Their nearest relatives, in the order edentata, include the sloth and the anteater.

The nine-banded armadillo is our mystery animal, *Dasypus novemcinctus*. It is the only armadillo found in the United States. It measures about 76 centimeters long and 15 centimeters high at the shoulder. It weighs about 6.4 kilograms.

Nine-banded Armadillos generally spend the day sleeping in burrows. They may have as many as 12 burrows located throughout their range. Each burrow consists of a labyrinth of tunnels that can be as long as eight meters. The armadillos will only share their burrows with members of the same sex.

At night, the armadillos emerge from the burrows to look for food. They are omnivorous, with insects forming most of their diet. Their strong sense of smell helps them detect food, and a long, sticky tongue draws out insects and larvae. Armadillos can eat more than 40,000 ants at one feeding.

The hard bony plates covering the armadillo's body are effective armor against attack. They are arranged in bands over the middle of the back and are attached to flexible skin. Fore and hind limbs have strong, curved claws for digging.

The nine-banded armadillo is the only armadillo species that can swim. It does this by inflating its stomach and intestines with air to keep it buoyant. It can also cross a small river or stream by walking on the bottom while holding its breath.

Mystery Animal 4—Walrus—*Odobenus rosmarus*

The walrus belongs to the carnivorous order of mammals known as pinnipeds. While its evolutionary history is still under debate, it can safely be said that the walrus probably evolved during the Oligocene Era from bear- or doglike ancestors of the North Pacific. The walrus's most prominent feature is its tusks. Tusks up to one meter in length are present in both males and females of the species.

The males are somewhat larger than the females. They average from 276 to 356 centimeters in length and can weigh 1200 kilograms or more. Both males and females tend to be a cinnamon brown color, but this can vary with age—younger walruses can be much darker in tone.

Walruses are considered "pagophilic" pinnipeds. This means "ice loving." Walrus populations are, therefore, circumpolar. However, their populations are not uniformly distributed. The highest density of walrus lies within 37 kilometers of the ice edge.

Walruses are bottom feeders. They disturb and physically alter the sea floor. Their habitat must include ocean bottoms that are covered with a wide variety of shellfish. Due to seasonal changes in ice coverage, the walrus is forced to follow food sources. Migration patterns follow the seasons.

The walrus population was believed to reach its lowest point in the mid-1950s. In the latest estimations, the walrus population is seeing a recovery. Current recorded populations number 200,000 to 230,000.

Mystery Animal 5—Western Honeybee—*Apis mellifera*

There has been a long relationship between human beings and the honeybee. Cave paintings in Europe show that people were harvesting honey as long as 8,000 years ago. The ancient Egyptians were the first beekeepers. They used the Western honeybee, our mystery species. This is the most widely used species in domestic beekeeping today. A second species, the Eastern honeybee, was also domesticated. This species is native to Asia.

The Western honeybee is a member of the insect order *Hymenoptera*. The bees are brightly colored and patterned to warn potential predators that they have a weapon to defend themselves. Their weapon is a modified ovipositor (egg-laying tube). Combined with a venom gland, the ovipositor becomes a stinger, or *aculeus*. When the hive is threatened, honeybees will swarm out and use the stingers to drive enemies away.

Honeybees are social insects. In the wild, they create elaborate nests called hives containing up to 20,000 individuals during the summer months.

Each bee in the hive belongs to one of three specialized groups, or castes: queens, drones, and workers. There is only one queen in each hive. She will live two to eight years and can lay more than 1,500 eggs a day. She is up to 20 millimeters larger than the other bees in the hive. Her stinger does not have barbs, so she can use it many times.

Drones live about eight weeks. Only a few hundred are ever present in the hive. Their sole function is to mate with a new queen.

Worker bees do all the different tasks needed to maintain the hive. They make up the vast majority of the hive's occupants. All worker bees are sterile.

Flower nectar is one of two food sources used by honeybees. The other is pollen. Both are gathered by field bees. They forage daily and bring back nectar and pollen to the hive for storage and conversion to honey.

There are four different species of honeybee in the world: Little honeybee (*Apis florea*), native to southeast Asia; Eastern honeybee (*Apis cerana*), native to eastern Asia; Giant honeybee (*Apis dorsata*), native to southeast Asia; and Western honeybee (*Apis mellifera*), native to Europe, Africa, and western Asia. The Western honeybee is our mystery species.

Mystery Animal 6—American Lobster—*Homarus Americanus*

Lobsters are members of the order Decapoda. They are crustaceans, characterized by hard exoskeletons and a jointed body. Lobsters are related to other crustaceans, including shrimp, green crabs, rock crabs, and barnacles. There are approximately 30 species of lobsters found around the world.

The American lobster, *homarus americanus,* is our mystery species. It is also known as the "true" lobster. It is found in cool waters from Canada to North Carolina. It has two strong front claws, which it uses for eating and tracking prey. Individuals can be gray, black, or brown, with a blue underbelly. Its eyes are carried on short stalks emerging from the front of the head. Lobsters are nocturnal, with highly developed senses of hearing and smell, and specially adapted eyesight.

American lobsters have five pairs of jointed legs. One or more are modified into pincers. The rest are used for swimming. The fan-shaped tail helps the lobster to propel itself backward at high speed.

Young lobsters grow by molting. A lobster will shed its shell up to 25 times during its first five years of life. Adult lobsters molt approximately once a year.

Lobsters are scavengers. They will feed on carrion, clams, snails, mussels, worms, and sea urchins. They will also eat other lobsters. The lobster's teeth are located in its stomach.

Other species of lobsters, such as the spiny lobster, are distant relatives. Spiny lobsters have no claws. Their shells are spine studded.

Information for the Student:
Animal Classification in Practice

In part 1 of this unit, you researched some of the major figures in the history of taxonomy. You also learned about how plant and animal classification helps people to understand the structure and behavior of living things.

In part 2 you will apply what you have learned to identify a mystery animal. You will study its characteristics and determine which class it belongs to, as well as which genus and species. You will then prepare a cladogram that shows your mystery animal and its nearest relatives.

You will work with a group to research the topic. You will then prepare a visual display to illustrate your findings. As you prepare to create your display, keep in mind the following questions:

- What information will I need to do my presentation?

- Where are the best places to find the information I need? What types of materials will be the most useful?

- What visual materials will best show the data and support my presentation? What text materials will I need to support my graphics?

- How can I present the information I find to make a clear, attractive, and exciting display?

Mystery Animal Card 1

- There are four species in my genus.
- I have a distinctive spotted coat.
- I am carnivorous.
- I have massive jaws and can crush bones with my teeth.
- I walk on my toes and have claws that cannot be retracted.
- I live south of the Sahara desert, and am not a leopard or jaguar.

Who am I?

_____

_____

Mystery Animal Card 2

- I live in the North Atlantic Ocean.
- I can weigh as much as a ton.
- I have tentacles with a distinctive club-shaped tip.
- I have the largest eyes of any animal in the world.
- I propel myself by expelling water from my mantle cavity.
- I am not an octopus.

Who am I?

_____

_____

Mystery Animal Card 3

- My name comes from the Spanish word *armado*, which means "one that is armed."
- I have a bony shell covering my body.
- I have a backbone.
- I am a good swimmer.
- I can be found in the southern United States.
- I am omnivorous.

Who am I?

_____

_____

Mystery Animal Card 4

- I live near the Arctic Circle.
- I have prominent tusks.
- My favorite food is shellfish.
- The males of my species are much larger than the females.
- I migrate with the seasons.

Who am I?

_____

_____

Mystery Animal Card 5

- I have an exoskeleton.
- I am highly social.
- I have a weapon that is a modified egg-laying tube.
- Only one individual female in my nest reproduces.
- I have a long history of domestication.
- I am native to Europe, Africa, and Western Asia. There are three other species that are similar to me in my genus. Only one other has been domesticated.

Who am I?

_____

_____

Mystery Animal Card 6

- I am nocturnal and very solitary in nature.
- I have an exoskeleton.
- I have two large claws.
- I live on the ocean bottom along the coast of North America.
- I am a scavenger.
- I am not a crab.

Who am I?

_____

_____

Organizational and Assessment Checklist for the Teacher

Lesson Component	Taught/Assessed by	Assessment Method
Introducing the Lesson —General Introduction • the kingdoms of life • identifying sources • how to prepare a bibliography		
The Language of Classification		• Review Worksheet 1-1 answers for completeness and student comprehension of the material
Linnaeus and the Development of Taxonomic Systems		• Review Worksheet 1-2 answers for student comprehension of the material • Review bibliography for completeness and relevance of sources
Other Systems of Taxonomy		• Review Worksheet 1-3 answers for student comprehension of the material • Review bibliography for completeness and relevance of sources
Writing a Persuasive Essay		• Review worksheet 1-4 • Assessment for Student Worksheet 1-4
Introduction to Part 2		
Identifying the Mystery Animal		• Review cooperative project checklists for all members of each group • Assess display cladogram for each group for accuracy of content (50%), dramatic impact (15%), and neatness (15%) • Assess group for quality of collaboration (10%) and participation by all members (10%)

Selected Suggested Resources/Bibliography

Items marked with an asterisk would be suitable for teacher background; all others would be for both teacher and student reference.

Web Sites

www.ucmp.berkeley.edu/history/linnaeus.html
     Brief yet thorough biographical data on Linnaeus.

www. sln.fi.edu/tfi/units/life/classify/classify.html
>   The Franklin Institute's comprehensive site devoted to animals and taxonomy. Offers a complete clearinghouse of related sites suitable for children.

http://www.ucmp.berkeley.edu/help/taxaform.html
>   Superb Web site for identifying animals by taxa.

http://tolweb.org/tree/phylogeny.html
>   The Tree of Life is a collaborative Internet project containing information about phylogeny and biodiversity. This site has more than 2,600 pages compiled by biologists from around the world. Each page deals with a different taxonomic order or species.

http://anthro.palomar.edu/animal/animal_2.htm
>   Excellent discussion and diagrams covering principles in classification.

http://school.discovery.com/sciencefaircentral/dysc/virtuallabs/bones/index.html
>   Interactive lab activity for classification of animals using types of bones.

http://www.pcisys.net/~dlblanc/taxonomy.html
>   Highly readable essay called "The ABCs of Taxonomy."

http://www.gwu.edu/~clade/faculty/lipscomb/Cladistics.pdf
>   Explains cladistic analysis through text and examples. Includes cladograms and multiple trees.

http://www.aber.ac.uk/education/PGCE/lbm96/
>   British Web site designed for high school students studying taxonomy.

http://www.csdl.tamu.edu/FLORA/aspt/asptcar1.htm
>   Describes careers in systematics and taxonomy.

http://www.bechly.de/glossary.htm
>   A glossary of terms used in systematics.

*http://www.indiana.edu/~ensiweb/lessons/whyclad.html
>   Presents a complete lesson plan, including worksheets.

http://town.morrison.co.us/dinosaur/tax-clad.html
>   Links to many taxonomy and cladistics pages.

http://www.nbii.gov/disciplines/systematics.html
>   More links to Web sites about systematics.

http://www.calacademy.org/research/systematics.html
>   Brief and to the point: why systematics is important, and how it is used.

http://www.itis.usda.gov/
>   Authoritative taxonomic information from the USDA.

http://nature.ac.uk/
>   A gateway coordinated by The Natural History Museum, London, dealing with all aspects of the natural world.

http://www.perspective.com/nature/index.html
>   Nature index organized according to the biological principles of taxonomy.

http://www.funet.fi/pub/sci/bio/life/intro.html
>   Taxonomic tree includes mammals, insects, birds, and plants.

http://www.fmnh.helsinki.fi/users/haaramo/index.htm
A compilation of various phylogenetic trees. Links to other taxonomic Web sites.

http://www.discoverlife.org/
Information about taxonomy, natural history, and distribution of many species. Includes tools to identify, map, and database species.

http://sis.agr.gc.ca/pls/itisca/taxaget?p_ifx=aafc
Searchable database of four kingdoms: plantia, animalia, fungi, monera.

http://www.eti.uva.nl/Database/
Advanced taxonomic trees, descriptions, synonyms.

http://www.anthro.washington.edu/Faculty/FacultyPages/dunnell/BOOK/book.html
Informative textbook—*Systematics in Prehistory* —online.

http://darwin.eeb.uconn.edu/systematics.html
Links to systematics resources.

http://www.biosis.org/zrdocs/zoolinfo/syst_tax.htm
Resources for systematics and taxonomy.

http://arnica.csustan.edu/boty3700/lectures/history.htm
History of the science of taxonomy from a Stanford University botany course.

Print Resources

Blunt, W. *Linnaeus: The Compleat Naturalist.* With an introduction by W. T. Stearn. Princeton, NJ: Princeton University Press, 2001.

*Crisci, Jorge Víctor, Joseph D. McInerney, and Patricia J. McWethy. *Order & Diversity in the Living World: Teaching Taxonomy & Systematics in Schools.* Reston, VA: National Association of Biology Teachers, c1993. Main QH83 .C74 1993.

*Forey, Peter L., et al. *Cladistics: A Practical Course in Systematics.* Oxford [England]: Clarendon Press; New York: Oxford University Press, 1993 (1995 printing). Herp QH83 .C485 1993.

Gee, Henry. *In Search of Deep Time: Beyond the Fossil Record to a New History of Life.* New York: Free Press, 1999. Pub QE721.2 .S7 G44 1999.

Goerke, H. *Linnaeus.* Translated from the German by D. Lindley. New York: Scribner, 1973. (First published as *Carl von Linné: Arzt, Naturforscher, Systematiker 1707–1778.* Stuttgart, Wissenschaftliche Verlagsgesellschaft, 1966. Grosse Naturforscher vol. 31. Re-pub. 1989.)

*Grande, Lance, and Olivier Rieppel, eds. *Interpreting the Hierarchy of Nature: From Systematic Patterns to Evolutionary Process Theories.* San Diego, CA: Academic Press, c1994. Main QH366.2 .I53 1994.

Jonsell, B. "Linnaeus in 20th Century Sweden." *Botanical Journal of the Linnean Society* 109 (1991): 515–528.

Margulis, Lynn. *Five Kingdoms: An Illustrated Guide to the Phyla of Life on Earth.* New York: W.H. Freeman, c1998. Main REF QH83 .M36 1998.

Margulis, Lynn. *Diversity of Life: The Five Kingdoms.* Berkeley Heights, NJ: Enslow Publishers, 1992.

* Minelli, Alessandro. *Biological Systematics: The State of Art*. London; New York: Chapman & Hall, 1993. Main QH83 .M565 1993.

Panchen, Alec L. *Classification, Evolution, and the Nature of Biology*. Cambridge [England]; New York: Cambridge University Press, 1992. Main & Herp QH83 .P35 1992.

Quicke, Donald L. J. *Principles and Techniques of Contemporary Taxonomy*. London; New York: Blackie Academic & Professional, 1993. Main QH83 .Q53 1993.

Savage, R. J. G. *Mammal Evolution: An Illustrated Guide*. New York: Facts on File Publications, 1986.

Stevens, Peter F. *The Development of Biological Systematics: Antoine-Laurent de Jussieu, Nature, and the Natural System*. New York: Columbia University Press, c1994. Main QH83 .S76 1994.

Tudge, Colin. *The Variety of Life: A Survey and a Celebration of All the Creatures That Have Ever Lived*. London; New York: Oxford University Press, 2000. Pub QH83 .T84 2000.

Wilson, Don E., and DeeAnn M. Reeder, eds. *Mammal Species of the World: A Taxonomic and Geographic Reference*. 2nd ed. Washington, DC: Smithsonian Institution Press, 1993.

Winston, Judith E. *Describing Species: Practical Taxonomic Procedure for Biologists*. New York: Columbia University Press, c1999. Main, Biodiv REF, & Herp QH83 .W57.

Show Dog or Show Dud?:
A Look at Genetic Inheritance

Object of This Lesson

In this unit, students will use library resources and a variety of research tools to explore the history of scientific discovery in the field of genetics and inheritance. They will learn, through a study of the ideas of Charles Darwin and Jean Lamarck, how people once viewed inheritance. By additional study of the work of Gregor Mendel, they will learn how experimentation led to a greater understanding of the mechanisms underlying heredity.

Students will then apply what they have learned to a study of domestic dogs. They will show how dogs evolved from wolves, and how various traits were selected for and bred through artificial selection.

This unit will support the following American Association for the Advancement of Science Benchmarks (p. 124):

- To recognize that small differences between parents and offspring can accumulate (through selective breeding) in successive generations so that descendants are very different from their ancestors.

- To recognize that information from fossils can shed light on changes in life forms over time.

Science Content Knowledge and Skills

Students will

- Describe verbally and in writing key points pertaining to Lamarck, Darwin, and Mendel's lives and theories;

- Describe verbally and in writing how Lamarck's theories differed from Darwin's;

- Explain how Darwin arrived at his idea of natural selection;

- Describe the experiments performed by Gregor Mendel on bean plants;

- Discuss how Mendel's experiments help us understand how genetic inheritance and natural selection work;

- Create a cladogram (family tree) for the canid family; and
- Create a Punnett's square to illustrate patterns of inheritance.

Information Literacy Knowledge and Skills

Students will

- Use a variety of different index types in order to locate material;
- Describe how they found and chose their resources;
- Evaluate the appropriateness of the research material;
- Identify three different types of media used to find the information required;
- Prepare a complete bibliography;
- Describe the difference between a primary and a secondary source;
- Explain how fact, point of view, and opinions are different from one another;
- Present information in a clear and organized manner;
- Integrate knowledge and information with that of others in the group;
- Help to organize and integrate the contributions of all the members of the group into information products;
- Participate actively in discussions with others to devise solutions to information problems that integrate group members' information and ideas; and
- Work with others to create and evaluate complex information products that communicate complex information and ideas.

Lesson Outline

This lesson is designed to be team-taught by a library media specialist and a science specialist. Before you introduce the lesson to students, decide which aspects of the unit will be presented by each member of the team. Decide who will assess student performance on each component of the unit. Use the checklist at the end of this chapter to assist you in organizing these aspects of teaching the unit.

Stimulate interest in the lesson by asking students: "Why is John's hair black, and Kim's hair blond? Why do giraffes have long necks, and kangaroos have pouches? Where does all the variety in plant and animals come from?"

Explain to students that you will be leading a research project into the origins of species. Explain that information they will find was very controversial in the 19th century, and, in some quarters, remains controversial today. Discuss the meaning of the terms *fact* and *opinion*. What is a theory? When does a scientific theory become a law?

Explain that the students will be conducting research into the subject by consulting many different types of sources. Ask students where they might find information on this topic. Create a list of possible sources of information on the blackboard.

Describe the differences between types of sources. Can students identify a primary source and a secondary source? Define each term. Direct students to keep a record of the definition.

Point out the list of sources you created on the blackboard. Ask students how they would find the appropriate materials in each category. Have you categorized the sources on the blackboard as the students mentioned them in discussion? Make sure students understand how to use the various indexing tools available in your information center.

Ask students what sources they would trust the most when reviewing information. Which sources would they trust the least? Offer possible suggestions: a museum or historical society Web site, a high school student's term paper posted on the Web, a local newspaper report, a scientific journal.

Discuss with students the meanings of various domain designations used on the Web. Have students identify the meanings of the following URL endings: .com, .gov, .org, .us. What do these designations tell Web users about the site? Have students create a glossary of domain designations for future reference.

Ask students how they will organize the information they collect. Brainstorm methods and materials to help in the organization and retrieval of data for this project. Introduce the concept of the bibliography. How will a bibliography help students keep track of their data? How else will a bibliography be useful?

Go over the proper format of bibliographical entries for different types of resources. Make sure students know which information is important for the bibliography and which information is not required. Also show students where the necessary information can be located, for example, in the front of a book or at the bottom of a Web page.

Explain to students that they will be analyzing patterns of inheritance in this unit. Describe how a Punnett's square (see below) is made and will be used to help in this analysis.

	B	b
B	BB	Bb
b	Bb	bb

Ask students if they have any questions about how to proceed with the first step of the project. Review as needed. It may be helpful to list all the steps required for completion of this project on the blackboard. Encourage students to use the checklist of steps on Research Project Checklist 1 (Student Worksheet 1-A) to keep track of their work.

Part 1—The Theory of Natural Selection

Background Information for the Teacher and Library Media Specialist

At the beginning of the 19th century, most people believed that living things did not change: all living things that existed now had existed, in the same form, since the beginning of time. This notion, however, was itself about to change. A French biologist, Jean Lamarck (1744–1829), proposed that animals do indeed evolve. The process, he thought, was stimulated by the actions of organs and appendages. For example, because a giraffe stretched its neck to reach high sources of food, eventually the neck grew. The acquired characteristic, a longer neck, would be passed on to the next generation.

Charles Darwin (1809–1882), like Lamarck, also believed that animals evolved. But Darwin did not agree with Lamarck's views on the mechanism behind the evolution. He developed a radical idea of his own. Darwin's view, as set out in his groundbreaking book, *On the Origin of Species by Means of Natural Selection* (1859), changed forever our view of biology.

Darwin and Scandal

The first edition of *On the Origin of Species* caused a sensation. The book sold out on its first day of publication. It went through six editions by 1872.

Many people were scandalized by Darwin's theories. They were widely considered to be a threat to the established order in Britain.

What did Darwin say that was so radical? He proposed that nature—not God—selects traits from the existing varieties found in plant and animal populations that offer the best chances of survival in a particular environment. The traits that allow a creature to exploit a niche and survive will be passed along to succeeding generations. Traits that do not confer an advantage will die with the individuals that possess them. Gradually, over several generations, new species will evolve from the common "parent."

Darwin's theory was not complete. There were aspects of inheritance that his theory did not explain. For example, if natural selection were the only process occurring, each generation should have less variation until all members of a population are essentially identical. That does not happen. Each new generation throws up new variations. Darwin was aware of this fact, but he did not understand what caused it.

Gregor Mendel

The first person to grasp the reason was Gregor Mendel (1822–1884). He was a German monk who conducted thousands of plant breeding experiments between 1856 and 1863. He discovered that parental traits combine in different ways in offspring. The recombination of traits allows for new variations to arise in successive generations.

It was not until the beginning of the 20th century that Mendel's pioneering work was rediscovered. Today, Darwin's and Mendel's advances continue to inform and direct scientific research.

Information for the Student: A Look at Genetic Inheritance

Imagine you are a Neanderthal. You are sitting around the campfire in your tribe's cave. Your dog, Woof, is sitting calmly at your feet, eating a scrap from your deer bone.

Is this portrait possible? Were ancient dogs like the dogs we know today? Or was Woof really Wolf, and are you about to be lunchmeat?

In this unit, you will explore how animals change over time, and how traits are passed from one generation to the next in plant and animal populations. You will get the chance to find out about how "man's best friend" evolved over thousand of years from wolves. And you will meet some of the giants in the field of science, including Charles Darwin and Gregor Mendel.

To succeed in this activity, you will need to do research using a variety of media and information sources. As you perform your research, keep in mind the following questions:

- Where are the best places to find the information I need? What types of materials will be the most useful?

- Is the source for my information reliable and accurate? Who is providing the information?

- Is the information relevant? How does this source help me answer the questions I am being asked or solve the problem I am being posed?

- How can I organize the information I find to make effective use of it when I need it?

At the end of this unit, you will need to prepare a bibliography of the sources you used to find the information you need. A bibliography is a summary of the documents you used. The materials are described using a standard format so that other people can find the same information you did and conduct their own research into the topic.

As you work, make sure you record the following information about your sources:

- The title of the book, article, video, or Web page you used;

- The complete name of the author;

- The publisher of the book or article, the producer of the video, or the Web site address;

- The date of publication or the date the material was produced; and

- The city in which the material was produced or published.

Collecting this information as you do your research will save you a great deal of time later. It will also help you locate information again if you need to refer back to something.

Keep all of your work on this project—notes, worksheets, and reference information—together in a file folder or binder.

Student Worksheet 2-1

Name _____ Date _____

Charles Darwin and the Origin of the Species

Charles Darwin was a British scientist who lived in the 19th century. He developed the idea of natural selection. It is one of the most important ideas in the history of science.

Use at least **six** different sources to find out more about Charles Darwin. Choose at least **three** different types of sources, such as reference books, periodicals, Web sites, or encyclopedias. Use at least **one** primary source.

Use the back of this sheet to make a list of questions to help guide your work. Check them off as you find the answers to each one. Write down the name and other bibliographic information of each source where you found the answers for future reference.

When you have completed your research, create a bibliography that lists all of your sources in alphabetical order. Highlight your primary sources. Then answer the following questions:

- Where did Charles Darwin travel on the H.M.S. *Beagle*?

  _____

- What was the name of the book Darwin published in 1859?

  _____

- Why did this book cause a scandal in England?

  _____

- Describe, in your own words, Darwin's theory of natural selection.

  _____

- What do you think about Darwin's theory? Do you think it makes sense? Do you agree or disagree with Darwin? Why?

  _____

Student Worksheet 2-2

Name _____ **Date** _____

Comparison of Lamarck and Darwin

Jean Lamarck was a French scientist who worked at the beginning of the 19th century. Like Charles Darwin, Lamarck was interested in evolution.

Use at least **four** different sources to find out more about Jean Lamarck. Use at least **one** primary source.

Using Research Project Checklist 1 (Student Worksheet 1-A) as a model, make a chart on the back of this worksheet to help organize your work. List the types of resources you will need. Check them off as you find and read them. Write down the name of each source and other details for future reference.

When you have completed your research, create a bibliography that lists all of your sources. Highlight your primary sources. Then answer the following questions:

- What did Lamarck think caused evolution?

  _____

- Did Lamarck's ideas influence Charles Darwin? How?

  _____

- Describe, in your own words, Lamarck's theory of acquired characteristics.

  _____

- Which of the following examples do you think would be an example of Lamarck's idea?:

  - A basketball player grows tall because she plays lots of basketball, which makes her stretch to the basket.

  - A basketball player grows tall because she has inherited genes for height from one or both parents.

    _____

- What do you think about Lamarck's theory? Do you think it makes sense? Do you agree or disagree with Lamarck? Why?

  _____

Student Worksheet 2-3

Name _____ **Date** _____

Gregor Mendel and the Processes of Inheritance

Gregor Mendel was a German monk. He developed the idea of genetic inheritance based on years of research into bean plants. His discovery ranks as one of the most important in the history of science.

Use at least **four** different sources to find out more about Gregor Mendel. Choose at least **three** different types of sources, such as references books, periodicals, Web sites, or encyclopedias.

When you have completed your research, create a bibliography that lists all of your sources. Then answer the following questions:

- Describe, in your own words, how Mendel used bean plants in his experiments.

  _____

- Can two tall bean plants produce seeds for short plants? Why or why not?

  _____

- How do you think Darwin would have reacted to news of Mendel's work?

  _____

- Draw a Punnett's square (see page 29) that shows the genotypes for two tall bean plants and their offspring.

Student Worksheet 2-4

Name _____ **Date** _____

Creating a Bibliography

For this project, you will use many different resources. Create a bibliography of the materials you used.

A bibliography follows a standard format. Use the examples below as models for each of your bibliography's entries.

Book:

Dennett, D.C. 1995. *Darwin's Dangerous Idea: Evolution and the Meanings of Life*. New York: Simon and Schuster.

Periodical or Journal Article:

Scientific American. 1994. Life in the Universe: special issue. 271(Oct.).

Web Site:

Biography of Gregor Mendel. Thinkquest. www.library.thinkquest.org/20465/mendl.html Last updated: June 8, 2004.

Video:

The Day the Universe Changed (episode #10, Worlds Without End). 1986. Owings Mills, MD: MPT-TV.

_____

_____

_____

_____

_____

_____

_____

Part 2—Inheritance of Traits via Selective Breeding in Dogs

Lesson Outline

In part 2 of this unit, students will apply what they have learned about natural selection to the study of dog evolution.

Stimulate interest in this portion of the unit by posting a variety of pictures of domestic dogs. Have students describe their own dogs and bring in photographs of their family pets for display.

Explain to students that they will be using what they have learned about natural selection to prepare an oral presentation on the history of dog evolution. Explain that the presentation will be given with a partner. Allow students to choose their partners for this project.

Explain that students will be conducting research into canine history. Ask students how they might search for this information on the Web. Introduce the concept of the search engine. Ask students to identify some search engines that might be useful as a starting point for this activity. Make a list of search engines on the blackboard.

Ask students what terms they might use to begin their search. Make a list of related terms, such as *dog evolution, canine history, dog genetics*, etc. Discuss how search engines operate. Encourage students to experiment with different terms in the search window of a search engine. Ask students to record how many sites each term or phrase returned. How can they successfully narrow their search to return only the most useful and pertinent sites?

Ask students what are the main questions they need to find answers for to succeed at this project. Encourage students to brainstorm questions such as, "What did the first dog look like?" Make a list of questions on the blackboard for students to use in organizing their projects.

Ask students how they will organize the information they collect so that they can present it to others. Introduce the concepts of cladograms and family trees. Ask them: How do scientists use these diagrams to classify animals? How will they help you keep track of your own data?

Tell students that note-taking during research is an excellent technique for recording and processing information. As they learn about this topic, they should keep notes of what they read in their journals or portfolios. They should use a highlighter to emphasize key points. They will use these key points later to organize their oral presentations.

Describe to students how scientific experimentation is used to classify animals. What kind of physical evidence might scientists use in their comparisons? Brainstorm a list of possibilities on the blackboard, for example, genetic information from bone or blood samples, skeletal structure from fossils and other bones, physical appearance. If the opportunity allows, you may wish to present a lab activity comparing actual specimens from a variety of related species to support this lesson.

Discuss with students the elements of a successful oral presentation. Explain that for the presentation, they will need to be able to speak clearly and make eye contact with the audience. Ask students to offer techniques, such as the use of cue cards or memorization of key parts of the speech, to make the presentation easier.

Point out that visual support material, such as graphics or charts, can contribute to a dynamic presentation. Also, emphasize that smooth transitions between presenters and a solid grasp of the topic material will contribute to their final grade.

Ask students if they have any questions about how to proceed with the project. Review as needed. It may be helpful to list all the steps required for completion of this project on the blackboard. Encourage students to use the checklist of steps to keep track of their work, as shown on Student Worksheet 2-5.

Student Worksheet 2-5

Name _____ Date _____

Show Dog or Show Dud?: Research Project Checklist 2

Use this checklist to help you organize and track your work on this project.

☐ My partner and I have made a list of questions we will need to answer for this project.

☐ I have divided tasks with my partner. My partner will be responsible for:

_____.

☐ I will be responsible for:

_____.

☐ We prepared a family tree that shows dog evolution.

☐ We have located guidelines for breeds from the American Kennel Club. This is where we found them:

_____.

☐ We have selected a single dog breed that we would like to use for our presentation. The breed is:

_____.

☐ I have taken notes about this topic in my journal.

☐ I have highlighted the following key points in my notes:

_____.

☐ My partner and I prepared each portion of our oral report using our notes as guidelines.

☐ My partner and I practiced presenting each portion of our oral report with each other.

☐ We have prepared the following visual support for our presentation:

_____.

Background Information for the Teacher and Library Media Specialist

Ancient Origins

All dogs—wild and domestic, extinct and living—belong to the canid family (family Canidæ). They first appeared in the fossil record about 40 million years ago, well before other carnivore families like cats or bears.

The first group of canids were called *Hesperocyons* (hess pur oh SYE onz). They evolved in North America about 40 million years ago. Fossil evidence suggests they resembled a cross between a weasel and fox. Hesperocyons became extinct about 15 million years ago.

The second group of canids, the *Borophagines* (bohr oh FAY jeens), were more like hyenas than dogs. They had huge jaw muscles and sturdy teeth. They became extinct about 2.5 million years ago.

The third group, the *Canines* (KAY nines), includes all living species of canines. They originated in North America. About 7 million years ago, some species crossed a land bridge to Asia. Canines today are found all over the world.

The Canine Family

Most of the 35 surviving species of canids belong to one of three main groups:

- South American zorros (foxes)

- Foxlike canines, including the red fox and its relatives

- Wolflike canines, including the coyote, jackals, wolves, and domestic dogs

Domestic Dogs

The history of domestic dogs began 20,000 years ago. First, Mesolithic Homo sapiens used dogs for hunting. Between 7,000 and 9,000 years ago, when people began herding livestock, dogs became important as guards.

Substantial fossil and genetic evidence proves that all dogs are the descendants of wolves. The two species are so similar that skeletons of the earliest dogs and their wild wolf cousins are very difficult to tell apart. Two key differences are:

- Dog skulls often have a more prominent "stop" (the break in the downward slope from the forehead to the tip of the nose).

- Dogs' teeth are squatter than those of similar-sized wolves.

Modern Dog Breeds

All of the nearly 400 dog breeds that exist today belong to a single species, *Canis familiaris*. Most of the variation comes from artificial selection for desirable traits by humans. For example, terriers were bred to kill rats, while pointers, setters, and hounds were all used in hunting. There is a dog bred for almost every purpose today.

Canine Timeline

1 million B.C.	The gray wolf family becomes the world's largest canine group.
100,000 B.C.	Gray wolves and subspecies are spread across Asia, the Middle East, Europe, and the Americas. Humans begin selecting wolves for puppy characteristics to be camp pets.
20,000 B.C.	Stone Age people breed dogs for their own purposes. Oldest evidence is a 14,000-year-old jaw with teeth of modern dog configuration found in Iraq.
7,000 B.C.	Egyptians develop dogs from their region, Tibet, and China.
4,500 B.C.	Fossils of the period are of pointer types, mastiffs, greyhounds, shepherds, and the wolflike spitz.
3,500 B.C.	Basic dog types reach Europe.
3,000 B.C.	Prototype pointer skeleton found in England exhibits evidence of greyhound and mastiff characteristics. Modern hunting dogs will evolve from these prototypes, called *Canis familiaris intermedius*.
2,000 B.C.	As the Neolithic period ends, most basic breeds are established.
A.D. 23–79	The Roman Pliny writes about hunters carrying dogs that stiffen and point their noses at game concealed in undergrowth.
100–1500	Though there are few breeds in any one region, breeds and strains number in the thousands worldwide.
1800–1900	Distinctive breed separations and refinements advance rapidly through kennel clubs and knowledge of scientific animal breeding. About 400 breeds exist today.

(Sources: National History Museum of Los Angeles County and *Encyclopedia Britannica*)

Information for the Student: Breeds of Dogs

In part 1 of this activity, you researched some of the major figures in the history of biology. You also learned about natural selection and genetic inheritance, and how they work to create evolutionary changes in species.

In part 2 of this project, you will apply what you have learned by preparing a presentation on the variety of breeds of domestic dogs. Dogs have evolved in two ways: by natural selection and by artificial selection.

To succeed in this activity, you will work with a partner to research the topic. You will do lab work or prepare visual displays to illustrate your findings. You will do an oral presentation that describes how modern dog traits evolved and how they relate to the original species characteristics. As you prepare for your presentation, keep in mind the following questions:

- What information will I need to do my presentation?

- Where are the best places to find the information I need? What types of materials will be the most useful?

- What visual materials will best show the data and support my presentation? Consider charts, illustrations, photographs, and diagrams.

- How can I organize the information I find to make a clear and exciting presentation?

Student Worksheet 2-6

Name _____ Date _____

Domestic Dog Family Tree

The first domestic dogs appeared about 20,000 years ago. They were descended from one of the oldest families of carnivores. Today, there are nearly 400 different types of dogs. They all belong to the same species.

Use a variety of resources to find out about the history of dog evolution. Draw a dog's family tree. Then answer the following questions.

- What is the closest living relative to the domestic dog?

  _____

- When did canids first appear in the fossil record?

  _____

- How did fossils help scientists learn about canine evolution?

  _____

- What is one main difference between dogs and wolves?

  _____

- How did natural selection affect the evolution of canids?

  _____

- What do you think accounts for the wide variety in dog types today? Explain your answer.

  _____

Student Worksheet 2-7

Name _____ **Date** _____

Selective Breeding Worksheet

The American Kennel Club recognizes nearly 400 different breeds of dogs.

Choose a type of dog using the American Kennel Club guidelines. Research its history. Compare the dog to what you have learned about its wild ancestors. Make a T-chart that shows the characteristics of wild dogs and the characteristics of your breed. Then answer the questions below.

- What traits have been emphasized in the dog you have selected? What traits have been eliminated?

_____

_____

_____

_____

- By what means were breeders able to affect the appearance and behavior of this breed of dog?

_____

_____

_____

_____

- Would the breed of dog you have selected have had a *better* or *worse* chance of survival in the wild than its ancestors? Why?

_____

_____

_____

_____

Assessment for Oral Presentation

Name _____ **Date** _____

Quality of Content

3 Message is clear to the audience. All visual displays support the presentation's main idea.

2 The audience is unsure of the main message of the presentation. Some visual displays support the main idea. Others detract from the message.

1 No clear message is presented. Visual support bears little relation to the main idea.

Organization

3 Presentation is well organized. Audience follows the presentation. Order of presentation makes sense.

2 Presentation is somewhat organized. Audience seems somewhat confused.

1 Presentation is not well organized. Visual and verbal presentations do not have a coherent order. Visual support interferes with the message. Audience is very confused and loses interest.

Style

3 Presentation is given with flair. Transitions between presenters and between types of material are handled smoothly. Visual displays are attractively prepared and dynamically presented.

2 Presentation is competent. Transitions are occasionally rocky. Visual displays are adequate but not dynamic.

1 Presentation is sloppy. Transitions between presenters and between types of materials are awkward and reveal a lack of preparation. Graphics are cursory and visually unexciting.

Mechanics

3 Entire presentation is smooth. Presenters seem to know their material and are confident of their facts. Spoken parts are expressive and easily understood by the audience.

2 Some parts of the presentation are smooth. Presenters are not entirely confident of their facts and are not able to answer questions readily. Spoken parts are not always understandable.

1 The presentation is not smoothly presented. The presenters are unsure of their material and are not easy to understand.

Organizational and Assessment Checklist for the Teacher

Lesson Component	Taught/Assessed by	Assessment Method
Introducing the Lesson —General Introduction • Identifying sources • How to prepare a bibliography • How to create a Punnett's square		• Review Worksheet 2-5
Charles Darwin and the Origin of the Species		• Review Worksheet 2-1 answers for student comprehension of the material • Review bibliography for completeness and relevance of sources
Comparison of Lamarck and Darwin		• Review Worksheet 2-2 answers for student comprehension of the material • Review bibliography for completeness and relevance of sources
Gregor Mendel and the Process of Inheritance		• Review Worksheet 2-3 answers for student comprehension of the material • Review bibliography for completeness and relevance of sources
Introduction to Part 2		
Domestic Dog Family Tree		• Review Worksheet 2-6 answers for student comprehension of the material • Review bibliography for completeness and relevance of sources
Selective Breeding Worksheet		• Review Worksheet 2-7 answers for student comprehension of the material • Review bibliography for completeness and relevance of sources
Oral Presentation		Assessment for Oral Presentation

Selected Suggested Resources/Bibliography

Items marked with an asterisk would be suitable for teacher background; all others would be for both teacher and student reference.

Web Sites

www.mendelweb.org/Mendel.html
Biographical information about Gregor Mendel and his experiments.

www.mnsu.edu/emuseum/information/biography/klmno/mendel_gregor.html
Biographical information about Gregor Mendel and his experiments.

www.biopoint.com/engaging/MENDEL/MENDEL.HTM
Biographical information about Gregor Mendel and his experiments.

mendel.imp.univie.ac.at/mendeljsp/biography/biography.jsp—23k—
Biographical information about Gregor Mendel and his experiments.

http://www.nhm.org/exhibitions/dogs/evolution/index.html
Kid-friendly discussion of dog evolution from the Los Angeles County Natural History Museum.

http://www.naturalworlds.org/wolf/history/wolf_history.htm
Good discussion of wolf evolution.

http://anthro.palomar.edu/evolve/evolve_2.htm
Clear discussion of Darwin's theory of natural selection.

anthro.palomar.edu/synthetic/synth_7.htm
Detailed discussion of the mechanisms at work in natural selection.

www.akc.org/breeds/index.cfm
American Kennel Club Web site.

Videos

Darwin's Revolution in Thought. 1995. Talk given by Stephen Jay Gould (No. 126). Available from Into the Classroom Video, 351 Pleasant Street, Northhampton, MA 01060 and from Amazon.com.

The Day the Universe Changed (episode #10, Worlds without End). 1986. Owings Mills, MD: MPT-TV.

God, Darwin and the Dinosaurs. 1989. Boston: WGBH Educational Foundation.

In the Beginning: The Creationist Controversy. 1994. Chicago: WTTW.

The Pleasure of Finding Things Out. 1982. Video interview with Richard Feynman. New York: Time/Life Video.

Print Resources

Berg, P., and M. Singer. *Dealing with Genes: The Language of Heredity.* Mill Valley, CA: University Science Books, 1992.

Berra, T. *Evolution and the Myth of Creationism: A Basic Guide to the Facts in the Evolution Debate.* Stanford, CA: Stanford University Press, 1990.

Burdansky, S. "The Truth About Dogs." *The Atlantic Online*, July 1999.

*Clough, M. "Diminish Students' Resistance to Biological Evolution." *American Biology Teacher* 56 (1994): 409–415.

Darwin, C. *On the Origin of Species by Means of Natural Selection*. London: J. Murray, 1859.

Dawkins, R. *Climbing Mount Improbable*. New York: W.W. Norton, 1996.

Dawkins, R. *The Selfish Gene, 1976/89*. Oxford: Oxford University Press, 1999.

Dennett, D. C. *Darwin's Dangerous Idea: Evolution and the Meanings of Life*. New York: Simon & Schuster, 1995

Futuyma, D. *Science on Trial: The Case for Evolution*. 2nd ed. Sunderland, MA.: Sinauer Associates, Inc., 1995.

Gamlin, Linda. *Eyewitness Science: Evolution*. New York: Dorling Kindersley, 1993.

*Gillis, A. "Keeping Creationism out of the Classroom." *BioScience* 44 (1994):650–656.

Goldschmidt, T. *Darwin's Dreampond: Drama in Lake Victoria*. Cambridge, MA: MIT Press, 1996.

Gould, S. J. "The Evolution of Life on the Earth." *Scientific American* 271 (October 1994): 85–91.

Lamarck, Jean. *Philosophie Zoologique*. Translated by H. Elliott. London: Macmillan, 1914.

Matsumura, M., ed. *Voices for Evolution*. 2nd ed. Berkeley, CA: National Center for Science Education, 1995.

Mayr, E. *This Is Biology: The Science of the Living World*. Cambridge, MA: Belknap Press of Harvard University Press, 1997.

*Mayr, E. *One Long Argument: Charles Darwin and the Genesis of Modern Evolutionary Thought*. Cambridge, MA: Harvard University Press, 1991.

*McComas, W., ed. *Investigating Evolutionary Biology in the Laboratory*. Reston, VA: National Association of Biology Teachers, 1994.

*McKinney, M. L. *Evolution of Life: Processes, Patterns, and Prospects*. Englewood Cliffs, NJ: Prentice Hall, 1993.

Mech, L. D., Dr. *The Wolf, Ecology and Behavior of an Endangered Species*. Garden City NY: USFWS, Natural History Press, 1970.

Morell, V. "The Origin of Dogs: Running with the Wolves." *Science* 276 (1997): 1647–1648.

Parker, Steve. *Science Discoveries: Charles Darwin and Evolution*. New York: Chelsea House Publishers, 1992.

Pickrell, J. "Dog DNA Study Yields Clues to Origins of Breeds." *National Geographic News,* May 20, 2004.

Scientific American. "DNA Study Traces Fido's Family Tree." *Scientific American* 271 (October 1994): Life in the universe: special issue.

Tiffin, L. *Creationism's Upside-down Pyramid: How Science Refutes Fundamentalism*. Amherst, NY: Prometheus Books, 1994.

Trut, L. N. "Early Canid Domestication." *American Scientist* 87, no. 2 (March–April 1999).

Vila, C., et al. "Multiple and Ancient Origins of the Domestic Dog." *Science* 276 (1997): 1687–1689.

Vila, C., J. E. Maldonado, and R. K. Wayne. "Phylogenetic Relationships, Evolution, and Genetic Diversity of the Domestic Dog." *Journal of Heredity* 90 (1999): 71–77.

Walsh, S., and T. Demere. *Facts, Faith and Fairness: Scientific Creationism Clouds Scientific Literacy.* Berkeley, CA: National Center for Science Education, 1993.

Weiner, J. *The Beak of the Finch: A Story of Evolution in Our Time.* New York: Alfred A. Knopf, 1994.

Wilson, E. *The Diversity of Life.* Cambridge, MA: Harvard University Press, 1992.

Sewers and Quarantines:
Public Health at Work

Object of This Lesson

In this unit, students use library resources and a variety of research tools to explore the history of public health. They will learn through a study of primary and secondary resources how improvements in sanitation helped reduce the spread of disease and increase life expectancy.

Students will then apply what they have learned to a study of the public health measures in place in their own community. Students will perform lab experiments to test water quality and assess the current state of local public health. Students would conclude this unit by writing to an appropriate government body or local media outlet to report their conclusions.

This unit will support the following American Association for the Advancement of Science Benchmarks (p. 206):

- To determine that sanitation measures such as the use of sewers, landfills, and quarantines are important in preventing the spread of disease-causing organisms.

- To recognize that improving sanitation has done more to save human life than any medical advances.

- To identify public health measures at work in their own community.

Science Content Knowledge and Skills

Students will

- Describe orally and in writing key points pertaining to public health measures including quarantine, waste disposal, water treatment, and basic sanitation;

- Describe orally and in writing how poor hygiene and public health measures contributed to disease epidemics such as bubonic plague, cholera, tuberculosis, typhoid, and SARS;

- Describe the advances made by key figures such as Florence Nightingale in improving public health;

• Describe public health measures in their own community;

• Analyze water quality using standard lab materials;

• Write a lab report;

• Explain how diseases such as bubonic plague are transmitted by insect vectors; and

• Explain how diseases such as typhoid or cholera are transmitted via contaminated water.

Information Literacy Knowledge and Skills

Students will

• Use a variety of different index types to locate material;

• Use telephone books and other directories to find information about their own community;

• Describe how they found and chose their resources;

• Evaluate the appropriateness of the research material;

• Identify three different types of media used to find the information required;

• Prepare a complete bibliography;

• Describe the difference between a primary and a secondary source;

• Access information from journals, diaries, government proceedings, the Internet, and newspaper accounts;

• Explain how fact, point of view, and opinions are different from one another;

• Present information in a clear and organized manner; and

• Express information creatively and evaluate strengths and weaknesses of creative presentations of information.

Lesson Outline

This lesson is designed to be team-taught by a library media specialist and a science specialist. Before you introduce the lesson to students, decide which aspects of the unit will be presented by each member of the team. Decide who will assess student performance on each component of the unit. Use the checklist at the end of this chapter to assist you in organizing these aspects of teaching the unit.

Stimulate interest in the lesson by asking students to imagine a city without running water or garbage disposal systems. How would people bathe, prepare food, or wash clothing? How would waste be disposed of?

Ask students to identify how running water and sewage systems, garbage disposal, and other aspects of public health help our towns and cities today. Make a chart on the blackboard comparing a modern city to a city of the past.

Explain to students that you will be leading a research project into how innovations in public health have had a huge impact on quality of life and human longevity.

Explain that the students will be conducting research into the subject by consulting many different types of sources. Ask students where they might find information on this topic. Create a list of possible sources of information on the blackboard.

Describe the differences between types of sources. Can students identify a primary source and a secondary source? Define each term. Direct students to keep a record of the definitions in their journals.

Point out the list of sources on the blackboard. Ask students how they would find the appropriate materials in each category. Make sure students understand how to use the various indexing tools available in your information center.

Ask students how they evaluate information they collect from the Internet. Discuss the concept of the "Ten Commandments"—or the Ten Cs—for evaluating Internet sources. A summary of the Ten Cs is provided on the student information handout later in the chapter.

Ask students how they will organize the information they collect. Brainstorm methods and materials to help in the organization and retrieval of data for this project. Reinforce the concept of the bibliography. How will a bibliography help students keep track of their data? How else will a bibliography be useful?

Go over the proper format of bibliographical entries for different types of resources. Make sure students know which information is important for the bibliography and which information is not required. Also show students where the necessary information can be located, for example, in the front of a book or at the bottom of a Web page. You may wish to give students Worksheet 2-4 (page 35) on this topic.

Explain to students that, after they have completed their research, they will work in groups to perform a dramatic scene based on what they have learned. Direct students to look for incidents or events that will lend themselves to dramatization while doing their research.

Ask students if they have any questions about how to proceed with the first step of the project. Review as needed. It may be helpful to list all the steps required for completion of this project on the blackboard. Encourage students to keep track of the steps by using Research Project Checklist 1 (Student Worksheet 1-A) as a model.

Part 1—Sewers and Quarantines: Public Health at Work

Background Information for the Teacher and Library Media Specialist

Today, most of us are aware of the role sanitation plays in preventing disease and keeping people healthy. But this wasn't always the case. Until the Industrial Revolution and the discovery of the germ theory of disease in the second half of the 19th century, hygiene and sanitation were considered niceties only for the rich.

From the Middle Ages to the 19th Century

From the Middle Ages on, most people lived in filthy and unhygienic conditions. The lack of sanitation contributed to average life spans of less than 20 years.

London, England, was a prime example. Right into the Victorian era, animals were slaughtered in central areas and their blood was allowed to run in the streets. Roadways were dumping grounds for refuse. Domestic animals such as hogs wandered freely. The wastes drew rats and other vermin.

Its sewers were nothing but open ditches sloped toward the Thames River. They quickly filled with garbage and human wastes. The effluvia overflowed onto streets and into houses and marketplaces throughout the city. The wastes soaked foundations, walls, and floors of living quarters. Wells and cisterns that supplied drinking water were frequently contaminated.

The stench was unbearable. The summer of 1858 was even referred to as the summer of "The Great Stink." Any resident who could fled the city for the fresher air of the countryside.

Indoors, sanitation was no better than outside. People lived in poorly lit, poorly ventilated, and extremely crowded buildings. Their bedding was infested with bedbugs and their woolen clothing harbored disease-bearing lice. The lack of fresh water made bathing difficult, and superstition reinforced aversion to bathing by suggesting that immersion actually caused disease—the coating of dirt on people's bodies was considered protective and healthful! Food scraps were thrown on the floor to dogs and cats. Flies were everywhere. Odors were often worse indoors than out, thanks to cesspits beneath the floors. The noxious fumes not only made life miserable, they caused asphyxiation or explosions because of buildups of methane gas.

The unsanitary conditions caused epidemic after epidemic of disease. People endured repeated incidences of epidemic and endemic diseases such as the bubonic plague (the Black Death), typhus, smallpox, and the White Death (tuberculosis). During the 15th century, the Black Death killed more than 60 million people, one-fourth of the world's population.

Contaminated water caused repeated outbreaks of cholera, typhoid, and other waterborne diseases for more than four centuries. Malaria, yellow fever, and tuberculosis were also rampant.

The Industrial Revolution

There was little improvement in the situation until the mid- to late 19th century. The Industrial Revolution increased the standard of living. Improvements such as cheap soap, inexpensive clothing, and better nutrition made a huge difference to the common person's health.

Advances in the understanding of infection also had a significant impact. Edwin Chadwick, a sanitary reformer of the era, experimented with obtaining clean water from lakes and reservoirs instead of the filthy Thames. He introduced a new Public Health Act that mandated proper disposal of human waste and condemned the collecting of nightsoil (human waste used for fertilizer) for profit. Centralized, covered sewers were begun in 1844. This program led to wholesale improvement of London's living conditions. Indoor plumbing and the introduction of Sir Thomas Crapper's toilet was the final link required to "flush away" London's problems.

Cleaning up the water supply was a huge step forward for public health. But there were other significant advances as well. Soaps, disinfectants, and pharmaceuticals were developed. Practices such as garbage collection, water treatment, the establishment of public health departments and regulations, and personal bathing became common. Child mortality dropped. The average life span increased.

The Science of Microbiology

Hospitals had always been dangerous places. But death during surgery plummeted during the 19th century as scientific principles of microbiology, introduced by Louis Pasteur, were applied to medicine. Doctors began following Dr. Joseph Lister's advice to wash their hands and use antiseptic techniques. People stopped dying from infection caused by the doctor. Women stopped dying of puerperal fever, a terrifying disease that struck during childbirth. It virtually disappeared once obstetricians began washing their hands between deliveries.

Florence Nightingale was one major force behind improving sanitation. Other significant figures during this period were Edward Jenner (1749–1823), Oliver Wendell Holmes (1809–1894), Ignaz Semmelweiss (1818–1865), Rudolf Virchow (1821–1902), Clara Barton (1821–1912), J. Henri Dunant (1828–1910), and Robert Koch (1843–1910).

Quarantines at Work

Another advance was in the practice of quarantine. Although quarantines had been implemented since the 14th century, it wasn't until 1878 that quarantines were enforced on a large scale. The United States, spurred by continued yellow fever epidemics, initiated federal quarantine legislation. The arrival of cholera from abroad in 1892 gave the government even greater authority. By 1921, all quarantine stations were under federal control. The quarantine practices helped prevent the spread to the general population of cholera and other diseases that accompanied the vast waves of immigration during this period.

The Modern Era

The 1930s saw a sharp rise in life expectancy. The introduction of antibiotics and continuing improvements in standards of cleanliness, hygiene, and sanitation all contributed to the increase. By the 1980s, people in the developed world took longer and healthier lives for granted. Healthy sanitation practices became a "given" in prosperous societies. Today, many public health efforts focus less on hygiene and more on avoidance of self-destructive behavior such as smoking, being overweight, and inactivity.

Yet we are not completely free of the scourges of the past. Food and waterborne diseases such as *E. coli* or Mad Cow Disease infection are on the rise. Venereal diseases have made a comeback, as has tuberculosis. Modern epidemics such as AIDS and SARS underscore the need for continued vigilance.

Practicing good sanitation and hygiene improves the quality of life. It reduces health care costs and leads to longer and more productive lives. Although at first blush it may seem unlikely, hand washing and clean water are actually the twin pillars of economic success.

Information for the Student: Public Health at Work

Imagine you live in the East End of London during the Middle Ages. People are dying in the streets, victims of the deadly Black Death. No one knows what causes the disease. No one knows how to prevent it. *What would you do?*

Today, we know that diseases such as the plague can largely be prevented by simple measures of sanitation. Although we now take it for granted that cleanliness is fundamental to maintaining health, in the past it was not always seen as important.

In this unit, you will explore how improvements in sanitation have had a huge impact on society. You will learn about how people used to live, and the ways that poor hygiene and sanitation contributed to epidemics such as cholera and typhoid. You will learn about the pioneers who began the sanitation revolution, and how advances in germ theory helped bolster their cause. You will also learn how your own community uses a variety of public health measures and rules to maintain the well-being of its citizens.

To succeed in this activity, you will need to do research using a variety of media and information sources. As you perform your research, keep in mind the following questions:

- Where are the best places to find the information I need? What types of materials will be the most useful?

- Is the source for my information reliable and accurate? Who is providing the information?

- Is the information relevant? How does this source help me answer the questions I am being asked or solve the problem I am being posed?

- How can I organize the information I find to make effective use of it when I need it?

- Which information will lend itself to dramatization?

- Did I record the sources of information I used so that I can create a bibliography?

Keep all of your work on this project—notes, worksheets, and reference information—together in a file folder or binder.

Student Worksheet 3-1

Name _____ **Date** _____

Yuk!

Until the latter part of the 19th century, most cities were filthy places. Sewage ran in open gutters in the streets. People often died of diseases caused by contaminated food or water.

Choose one of the following three cities to study: Paris, London, or New York.

Use at least **six** different sources to find out more about the city's past. What was life like in your city? How were the following handled?

- Sewage

- Garbage disposal

- Infectious diseases

What steps were made that improved public health?

Choose at least **three** different types of sources, such as reference books, periodicals, Web sites or encyclopedias. Use at least **two** primary sources such as contemporary newspaper accounts, diary entries, or biographies.

Use the back of this sheet to record the dates when various public health measures were implemented. Write down bibliographic information for each source you use for future reference.

When you have completed your research, create a bibliography that lists all of your sources in alphabetical order. Highlight your primary sources. Then create a timeline that shows the history of your city's improvements.

Student Worksheet 3-2

Name _____ Date _____

It's an Epidemic!

Cholera   Bubonic Plague   Tuberculosis   Typhoid
SARS   Puerperal Fever   Influenza

An epidemic is a widespread outbreak of disease. There have been epidemics in many places in all times throughout history.

Many epidemics could have been avoided by using better sanitation. Choose one of the diseases listed above. **Research** its history. Use at least **four** different sources. Use at least **one** primary source.

When you have completed your research, create a bibliography that lists all of your sources. Highlight your primary sources. Then answer the following questions:

- What organism causes this disease?

  _____

- How does the disease spread?

  _____

- When and where were there major outbreaks of this disease?

  _____

- What public health measures could have reduced the severity of this epidemic?

  _____

- Could another epidemic of this disease happen again today? Why or why not?

  _____

  _____

  _____

  _____

Student Worksheet 3-3

Name _____ Date _____

Acting Up

For this activity, you will work with a group to create a dramatic performance based on your research.

Choose your partners. Decide on a topic for your dramatic scene. Make sure your scene has the following elements:

- **Protagonist:** Your central character.

- **Motivation:** Establish a personality for your protagonist and a reason why he or she behaves in a certain way.

- **Conflict:** The central reason for your drama. What does the protagonist want or need to do? Why? What is stopping him or her from achieving that goal?

- **Resolution:** Your drama should end with a solution for the conflict.

Write a script for your play. List all the props you will need to act out your play.

Present your play to your classmates. When you have finished your production, allow your classmates to give you feedback on the following topics:

- How strong was the information presented in this play? Was it factual?

- How polished was the presentation?

- Did the play make sense? Were the main characters clearly defined? Were their motivations presented well?

Assessment for Dramatic Presentation

Name _____ **Date** _____

Quality of Content

3   Message is clear to the audience. All action supports the presentation's main idea.

2   The audience is unsure of the main message of the presentation. Some of the action supports the main idea. Others detract from the message.

1   No clear message is presented. Drama bears little relation to the main idea.

Organization

3   Presentation is well organized. Audience follows the presentation. Order of presentation makes sense.

2   Presentation is somewhat organized. Audience seems somewhat confused.

1   Presentation is not well organized. Drama does not have a coherent order. Audience is very confused and loses interest.

Style

3   Presentation is given with dramatic flair.

2   Presentation is competent.

1   Presentation is sloppy.

Mechanics

3   Entire presentation is smooth. Presenters seem to know their material and are confident of their facts. Spoken parts are expressive and easily understood by the audience.

2   Some parts of the presentation are smooth. Presenters are not entirely confident of their facts and are not able to answer questions readily. Spoken parts are not always understandable.

1   The presentation is not smoothly presented. The presenters are unsure of their material and are not easy to understand.

Part 2—Public Health in Your Community

Background Information for the Teacher and Library Media Specialist

In part 2 of this unit, students will apply what they have learned about hygiene and sanitation to their own community. They will perform lab experiments to test the water and write up detailed lab reports about them. (Sources for supplies are listed at the end of this chapter.) They will do a study of how public health responsibilities are apportioned and how your community stacks up against others. Finally, they will communicate their findings to a media outlet or to local government officials.

Lesson Outline

Stimulate interest in this portion of the unit by asking students what public health measures are in force in your community. Ask students if they know what agencies oversee various aspects of public health, such as waste disposal, water treatment, infectious disease control, etc. Ask students how they might find out this information. Write the ideas they brainstorm on the blackboard.

Explain to students that they will be exploring public health right here in their own community by doing research and by doing a lab experiment to study water quality. Allow students to choose a partner for this project.

Tell students that note-taking during research is an excellent technique for recording and processing information. As they learn about this topic, they should keep notes of what they read in their journals or portfolios. They should use a highlighter to emphasize key points, which they will use later to organize their oral presentations.

Ask students what procedures they will need to do to test water quality. What materials will they need? How will they write a lab report detailing the findings of their experiment? Make a list of steps for performing a scientific experiment on the blackboard.

Tell students that after they have completed their research and their lab experiments, they will "grade" their community on its success in implementing proper public health measures. They will communicate their findings either to a local media outlet or to the appropriate government agency.

Ask students in what format they will deliver this information. Make sure students know how to write a standard business letter.

Ask students if they have any questions about how to proceed with the project. Review the components of this project as necessary. Encourage students to keep track of the steps by using Research Project Checklist 1 (Student Worksheet 1-A)

Information for the Student: Public Health at Work

In part 1 of this activity, you researched the history of public health. You also learned about diseases and epidemics, and how public health measures can reduce the incidence of disease.

In part 2 of this project, you will apply what you have learned to a study of your own community's public health practices.

To succeed in this activity, you will work with a partner to research the topic. You will do lab work to analyze your community's water. You will assess the performance of your community's public health program. Then you will communicate your findings to the appropriate government agency or a local media outlet. As you engage in your project, keep in mind the following questions:

- What information will I need for this project?

- Where are the best places to find the information I need? What types of materials will be the most useful?

- What visual materials will best show the data and support my project? (Consider charts, illustrations, photographs, and diagrams.)

- What materials will I need to conduct my experiment?

- Are my lab report and business letters clearly written, concise, and accurate?

- Have I provided adequate documentation to support my conclusions?

Student Worksheet 3-4

Name _____ **Date** _____

Who Does What?

Find out what agencies or departments are responsible for the following areas of public health and safety in your community. Make a contact list complete with phone and fax numbers for each department.

1. Garbage collection _____

   _____

2. Sewer maintenance _____

   _____

3. Water treatment _____

   _____

4. Infectious disease control _____

   _____

5. Vermin and pest control _____

   _____

6. Air quality _____

   _____

7. Smoking by-laws _____

   _____

8. Restaurant food inspection _____

   _____

9. Chemical spills _____

   _____

10. Animal control/leash laws _____

   _____

Student Worksheet 3-5

Name _____ Date _____

How Does Your Community Rate?

Review the practices and by-laws of your community in the following categories. How does your community compare to what you know about good public health? Is your community doing enough? What else should your community do to improve public health?

Rate your community's performance in each of the following areas. Use a score of 1 to 5, with 5 being "poor" and 5 being "outstanding." Be sure that you can provide hard data to support your ratings.

For each topic, suggest one change that your community could make that would improve public health.

Topic	Rating	Suggested Change
Garbage collection		
Sewer maintenance		
Water treatment		
Infectious disease control		
Vermin and pest control		
Air quality		
Smoking by-laws		
Restaurant food inspection		
Chemical spills		
Animal control/leash laws		

Student Worksheet 3-6

Name _____ **Date** _____

Water Quality Lab

Use the materials provided by your teacher to conduct experiments on the quality of water in your community. Write up a complete lab report. Then answer the following questions:

- How many tests did you perform? _____

- For what substances did you test? _____

- What were the findings for each test?

_____

_____

_____

_____

_____

_____

_____

_____

_____

- In your own words, describe the water quality of the sample(s) you collected.

_____

- How would you rate the quality of the *data* you collected? In other words, how well do you think you performed this experiment? Are your data accurate? Would you rely on your data to make a decision that might affect public health? Why or why not?

_____

Student Worksheet 3-7

Name _____ **Date** _____

Communicating Your Findings

For this part of the unit, you will write a letter to a government official or a media outlet about your community's public health practices.

Decide to whom you wish to write. List your choice(s) and the reasons for your choice(s) here:

_____

_____

Find the address(es) for your choice(s). Write them here:

_____

Next, write your letter. Make sure it follows standard business correspondence format. Your letter should include:

- Your school name and address;
- The date;
- The recipient's name and address;
- Who you are, and what your school project was;
- What your class found out while doing the project;
- Your assessment of the public health practices of your town in the specific area on which you are commenting;
- Data that support your assessment;
- Recommendations for improvement, if needed, or congratulations; and
- Your signature.

Use the back of this worksheet to answer the following questions:

- Do you think your correspondent will reply to your letter? Why or why not?
- Do you think your correspondent will take any action as a consequence of receiving your letter? Why or why not?

Information for the Student:
The Ten Cs for Evaluating Internet Sources

- **Content**

  What is the purpose of the Web site or page? What is the date of the document?

- **Credibility**

  Who is the author of the document? Who is the publisher of the Web site? What is the URL

  extension? What do the extensions .edu, .com, .gov, and .org stand for, and how do they help you evaluate the credibility of this source?

- **Critical Thinking**

  Are you using your critical thinking skills as you study the document, or are you simply accepting the information as it is provided?

- **Copyright**

  Are the materials you are using from the Internet copyrighted, or are they in the public domain? How can you tell? Do you know the rules for using material that is copyrighted?

- **Citation**

  Can you cite this material correctly in your bibliography?

- **Continuity**

  How long has this Web site been operating? Will it continue to be maintained and updated? When was it last updated? Is information from this source current or outdated? Will you be able to access this material in the future? Will there be a charge in the future to access this material?

- **Censorship**

  Is this material available to all? Is the material being monitored (such as by a moderator on a discussion group), and if so, what is being deleted before you see it? Some sites do not allow searches that use certain proscribed words, for example, racial slurs or obscenities. Does the search engine or index in this site prohibit searching for certain words?

- **Connectivity**

  Is this Web site viewable by all, or does it require certain Web browsers or other software?

- **Comparability**

  Does this source have an equivalent print or CD-ROM, or is the Internet version a condensed version of another resource (such as a newspaper)? How can you compare your Internet data to other materials, or to earlier versions?

- **Context**

  What is the context for the information being provided? For example, is the medical advice intended for doctors or for the general public?

Organizational and Assessment Checklist for the Teacher

Lesson Component	Taught/Assessed by	Assessment Method
Introducing the Lesson —General Introduction • Identifying sources • How to prepare a bibliography • Present Ten Cs for evaluating Internet sources		
Yuk!		• Review Worksheet 3-1 timeline for student comprehension of the material • Review bibliography for completeness and relevance of sources
It's an Epidemic!		• Review Worksheet 3-2 answers for student comprehension of the material • Review bibliography for completeness and relevance of sources
Acting Up		• Assessment for Dramatic Presentation
Introduction to Part 2 • Note-taking skills • How to perform a science experiment • How to write a lab report • How to write a standard business letter		
Who Does What?		• Review Worksheet 3-4 answers for student comprehension of the material and relevance of sources
How Does Your Community Rate?		• Review Worksheet 3-5 answers for student comprehension of the material
Water Quality Lab		• Mark lab report • Review Worksheet 3-6 for student comprehension of material
Communicate Your Findings		• Review letter—compare to elements identified on student Worksheet 3-7 to ensure all elements are present • Review answers to student Worksheet 3-7

Selected Suggested Resources/Bibliography

Items marked with an asterisk would be suitable for teacher background; all others would be for both teacher and student reference.

Laboratory Materials

There are many materials available for testing fresh and tap water. For this lab activity, we suggest you use a prepared kit that includes all the materials for the number of students in your class and complete instructions.

All of the suggested materials listed below are available from:

NASCO
901 Janesville Ave.
PO Box 901
Ft. Atkinson, WI 53538-0901
800-558-9595
www.eNASCO.com

- Water Monitoring Kit. Product # SB33597M. Approx. cost—$28.95

- The Tap Water Tour. For 35 students. Product #SB18965M. Approx. cost—$55.00

- The Testab Water Investigation Kit. 100 tests. Product # SB31250M. Approx. cost—$165.00

- Waterworks School Test Kit. 60 tests for nine different parameters. Product # SB31266M. Approx. cost—$90.00

- Qualitative Introduction to Water Pollution Kit #19. For 50 students. Product #SA08211M. Approx. cost—$120.00

- Water Quality Test Kit. 100 tests for six parameters. Product # SB35045M. Approx. cost—$165.00

- Environmental Monitoring Test Kit. 100 tests for six parameters. Product #SB35044M. Approx. cost—$135.00

- Thermal and Sewage Pollution Kit. For 30 students working individually. Product #SB29034M. Approx. cost—$90.00

Web Sites

http://www.uwec.edu/Library/Guides/tencs.html
   McIntyre Library at the University of Wisconsin-Eau Claire. Source document for "Ten Cs for Evaluating Internet Sources." Index for the library also includes several other useful guides, such as how to find books and articles on the Internet, how to do a Boolean search, and how to evaluate search engines.

http://www.swopnet.com/engr/londonsewers/londontext1.html
   Provides a vivid three-part article on the history of London's sewers.

http://scholars.nus.edu.sg/landow/victorian/science/health/healthov.html
   Complete site for Victoriana has articles on a variety of science and health topics focusing on England.

http://156.145.78.54/htm/home.htm
> The Living City Home page. Traces the history of New York City, with pages devoted to public health. Lots of links to related pages.

http://www.cdc.gov/ncidod/dq/history.htm
> Centers for Disease Control. Infectious disease information, epidemic data.

http://www.haciendapub.com/faria5.html
> History of quarantine practices.

Print Resources

Blackmar, Elizabeth. "Accountability for Public Health: Regulating the Housing Market in Nineteenth-Century New York City." In *Hives of Sickness: Public Health and Epidemics in New York City,* edited by David Rosner. New Brunswick, NJ: Rutgers University Press, 1995.

Broadman, Estelle. "New York City Department of Health, Periodicals and Serials Published, 1866–1939." *Special Libraries* XXXI (1940): 23–29, 59–64.

Cleaner Magazine. Published by Cole Publishing Inc., POB 220, Three Lakes WI 54562, 800-257-7222 or 715-546-3346.

Cohen, Paul E., and Robert T. Augustyn. *Manhattan in Maps, 1527–1995.* New York: Rizzoli, 1997.

Duffy, John. *A History of Public Health in New York City: 1866-1966.* New York: Russell Sage Foundation, 1974.

Duffy, John. *The Sanitarians: A History of Public Health in America.* Urbana and Chicago: University of Illinois Press, 1990.

Hiatt, N. T., Jr. "A History of Life Expectancy in Two Developed Countries." *The Pharos* 55, no. 2 (1992): 3.

Homberger, Eric. *The Historical Atlas of New York City.* New York: Henry Holt, 1994.

Hood, C. *722 Miles: The Building of the Subways and How They Transformed New York.* New York: Simon & Schuster, 1993.

Koppel, Gerard T. *Water for Gotham: A History.* Princeton, NJ: Princeton University Press, 2000.

Plunz, Richard. *A History of Housing in New York City: Dwelling Type and Social Change in the American Metropolis.* New York: Columbia University Press, 1992.

*Tarr, Joel A. *The Search for the Ultimate Sink: Urban Pollution in Historical Perspective.* Akron, OH: University of Akron Press, 1996.

Do Diets Work?:
Nutrition, Exercise, and Metabolism

Object of This Lesson

In this unit, students use library resources and a variety of research tools to take a critical look at nutrition, exercise, and human metabolism. They will learn through an examination of academic and popular information resources how judicious weight management plays a role in maintaining health.

Students will then apply what they have learned to perform a literature review of popular diets and a scientific study of their own habits. They will use calorie counters to record and analyze their own food intake and energy expenditures. They will review some of the popular diet books, plans, and supplements available in the mass market and compare their claims to what students know about safe and healthy weight loss techniques. They will conclude this unit by preparing an information brochure on healthy diet and exercise for distribution to the school population.

This unit will support the following American Association for the Advancement of Science Benchmarks (p. 145):

- To determine that the amount of food energy a person requires varies with body weight, age, sex, activity level, etc.

- To recognize that exercise is important to maintain a healthy body and healthy weight.

- To recognize that dietary habits and personal behavior can affect human health.

Science Content Knowledge and Skills

Students will

- Define the terms *calorie* and *metabolism;*

- Describe orally and in writing how a healthy body weight is maintained through a combination of adequate exercise and calorie intake;

- Describe some health consequences caused by having a too high or too low body weight;

- Identify some healthy and unhealthy foods;

- Determine a healthy body weight and level of daily exercise for themselves;

- Collect, record, and present scientific data in an appropriate format;

- Explain how diet and exercise work together to determine weight gain or loss; and

- Explain why extremely low-caloric, low-fat, or low-carb diets can be potentially dangerous.

Information Literacy Knowledge and Skills

Students will

- Use a variety of different index types to locate material;

- Use periodicals, popular science and health guides, government resources, and scientific documents to collect information;

- Describe how they found and chose their resources;

- Evaluate the appropriateness of the research material;

- Judge and support judgments of the degree of inaccuracy, bias, or misleading information in information sources;

- Identify three different types of media used to find the information required;

- Prepare a complete bibliography;

- Explain how fact, point of view, and opinions differ from one another;

- Present information in a clear and organized manner;

- Express information creatively and evaluate strengths and weaknesses of creative presentations of information;

- Use information for personal interest; and

- Respect information property rights by citing information responsibly.

Lesson Outline

This lesson is designed to be team-taught by a library media specialist and a science specialist. Before you introduce the lesson to students, decide which aspects of the unit will be presented by each member of the team. Decide who will assess student performance on each component of the unit. Use the checklist at the end of this chapter to assist you in organizing these aspects of teaching this unit.

Stimulate interest in the lesson by sharing with students that a recent study by the Centers for Disease Control (CDC) found that 25 percent of students were overweight or at serious risk of becoming so. Forty-three percent were trying active weight loss and a further 19 percent were working to keep their weight stable. Explain that excessive weight has been shown to lead to serious problems such as diabetes and heart disease. It can also reduce the quality of life by interfering with energy levels and mobility, and by affecting self-esteem. Too low body weight also causes health problems such as excess fatigue, poor memory and concentration, and kidney damage.

Ask students if they are familiar with any popular diet regimes. Write the names of the diets, for example, Atkins or South Beach, on the blackboard. Can students say conclusively whether or not any of these programs are safe and effective?

Explain to students that you will be leading a research project into whether popular diets such as the ones listed on the board actually work. Explain that the students will be conducting research by consulting many different types of sources. Ask students where they might find information on this topic. Create a list of possible sources of information on the blackboard.

Describe the differences between types of sources. Which sources would be the most reliable for finding this information? Which sources might be most likely to offer inaccurate or misleading information? Explain to students how they can determine the validity of any information by evaluating the aims of the provider. Is the provider a nonprofit health organization or a seller of diet supplements?

Point out the list of reliable sources on the blackboard. Ask students how they would find the appropriate materials in each category. Make sure students understand how to use the various indexing tools available in your information center.

Ask students how they will organize the information they collect. Brainstorm methods and materials to help in the organization and retrieval of data for this project. Introduce the concept of the bibliography. How will a bibliography help students keep track of their data? How will preparing the bibliography properly safeguard against misleading information? How else will a bibliography be useful?

Go over the proper format of bibliographical entries for different types of resources. Make sure students know which information is important for the bibliography and which information is not required. Also show students where the necessary information can be located, for example, in the front of a book or at the bottom of a Web page.

Explain to students that, after they have completed their research, they will review the safety and effectiveness of some popular diet plans. They will determine whether or not each diet plan offers a safe and effective method of weight loss.

Ask students if they have any questions about how to proceed with the first step of the project. Review as needed. It may be helpful to list all the steps required for completion of this project on the blackboard. Encourage students to use Research Project Checklist 1 (Student Worksheet 1-A) as a model for creating their own checklists.

Part 1—Nutrition, Exercise, and Metabolism

Background Information for the Teacher and Library Media Specialist

The pace at which an individual body engine operates is called the *metabolism*. Metabolic processes include the creation of some materials or forms of energy, such as heat, muscle, proteins, RNA, hair, nails, enzymes, storage fat, and bones. They also include the breaking down of materials, such as food and storage fat. Both the creation process (anabolic metabolism) and the breaking down process (catabolic metabolism) happen concurrently, all the time.

The energy for the process is provided by food. Food energy is measured in *calories*. A calorie is the unit of heat equal to the amount of heat required to raise the temperature of one kilogram of water by one degree Celsius at one atmosphere pressure.

Three factors contribute to overall metabolic rate. The first is Basal Metabolic Rate (BMR). This is the number of calories a body burns while at rest. The BMR accounts for about 60 percent of all energy used by the body.

Additional physical activity accounts for another 30 percent of energy used. The third factor is called *dietary thermogenesis*. This term refers to the energy used to digest and process food. It accounts for about 10 percent of energy needs.

Factors Affecting Basal Metabolic Rate

Many different contributors affect metabolism. First, and most important, is genetic inheritance. Some people have naturally slower or faster metabolisms than others. Second is gender. Because men have a greater muscle mass and a lower body fat percentage, they generally have a higher basal metabolic rate.

BMR is also affected by age, weight, and height. Younger people have higher BMRs than older people. The BMR usually drops 2 percent per decade after age 20. Heavier and taller people tend to have higher BMRs than lighter or shorter people.

How much body fat you have and what you eat will also affect the BMR. People with a higher body fat percentage generally have a lower BMR than those with a lower body fat.

An abrupt reduction in calories consumed can reduce BMR by up to 30 percent. Other factors include body temperature and overall health, external temperature, hormone levels, and amount of exercise.

Your BMR determines how many calories you need to sustain your life functions. If you take in more than this number of calories, you will gain weight. If you take in less, you will lose weight. While it is true that some foods get stored as fat more easily than others, it's just not possible to circumvent the laws of thermodynamics and energy balance. To burn fat you must create a calorie deficit between calories in and calories out. This calorie deficit forces your body to use stored body fat to find the required energy and make up the deficit.

Teenagers and Health

Maintaining a healthy weight is extremely important to long-term health. Yet teenagers today are exhibiting an alarming trend: According to the 1999–2000 National Health and Nutrition Examination Survey, the percentage of teenagers and children who are overweight continues to increase. Among children and teens ages 6 to 19, 15 percent (almost 9 million) are overweight. This is triple the percentage in 1980. In addition, more than 10 percent of children between ages two and five are overweight. Type 2 diabetes, associated with obesity and previously considered an adult disease, has increased dramatically in children and adolescents.

In the short term, overweight teens suffer from social discrimination, low self-esteem, and depression. In the long run, they have a 70 percent chance of becoming overweight or obese adults. This puts them at risk for a number of health problems including heart disease, high blood pressure, and some forms of cancer.

Frequently, American teenagers use unhealthy means to try to control their weight. According to the Centers for Disease Control (CDC), around one-third of females and 20 percent of males who are trying to lose weight fast use medications or laxatives. Girls who are trying to lose weight are also 40 percent more likely to smoke than females who are not. Only 25 percent of teens were consuming five or more servings of fruit and vegetables daily.

Learning how to control one's weight safely and effectively is therefore a priority for improving the prospects for teenager's health. The first step is to assess what is a proper weight.

The Body Mass Index

The Body Mass Index (BMI) is an excellent tool for determining a person's optimum weight based on height, age, and gender. The BMI for adults is expressed as a ratio. To calculate BMI, follow these steps:

1. Write down the weight in pounds.

2. Divide the weight by height in inches.

3. Divide the answer from step 2 by the height in inches.

4. Then multiply the answer from step 3 by 703.

5. The resulting answer is your BMI.

To calculate using metric measurements, follow these steps:

1. Write down your weight in kilograms.

2. Divide your weight by your height in centimeters.

3. Divide the answer from step 2 by your height in centimeters.

4. Then multiply the answer from step 3 by 10,000.

5. The resulting answer is your BMI.

Children's BMI

Children's body fat percentages change as they grow. Also, girls and boys differ in their body fat percentages. As a result, the BMI for children, also referred to as BMI-for-age, is plotted on gender specific growth charts. These charts are used for children and teens 2 to 20 years of age. Where the BMI lies on the chart can then be expressed as a percentile. You can obtain a copy of the charts online at kidshealth.org/teen/food_fitness/dieting/bmi.html or from a health practitioner in your community.

The standards for children are:

Underweight BMI-for-age	< 5th percentile
At risk of overweight BMI-for-age	85th percentile to < 95th percentile
Overweight BMI-for-age	> 95th percentile

Teenagers, whose bodies are still growing, should use BMI figures cautiously. Make sure students refer to information that is suitable for their age when analyzing their own health status and practices.

To Gain or to Lose?

Once your BMI has been determined, you can clearly see if you need to lose or gain weight. For many people in our society, losing weight is the goal. Doing so is simple in theory, but difficult in practice.

There are about 3,500 calories in a pound of stored body fat. To lose one pound of fat, you must create a 3,500-calorie deficit. The deficit can be achieved either by calorie-restriction alone or by a combination of fewer calories in (diet) and more calories out (exercise). The combination of diet and exercise is best for lasting weight loss.

Dangers in Calorie Cutting

Cutting calories too low can be counterproductive to weight loss. Your body thinks there is a food shortage. It slows down your metabolism to stretch the calories. Reduced calories may also decrease thyroid output, causing loss of lean body mass. Too few calories invariably slow down weight loss or stop it completely.

Losing weight too quickly can also be counterproductive. The average healthy human body simply will not shed more than about two pounds of fat per week. But it *will* shed water. This is what most rapid weight loss is—just water. The weight will return as soon as the water is replaced.

Reducing calorie intake can also compromise nutrition. It can be difficult to get adequate nutrients from a typical Western diet. Cutting out too many foods in an effort to reduce calories may also mean cutting out essential vitamins and nutrients.

If you want to lose fat, a useful guideline is to reduce your calories by at least 500, but not more than 1,000 below your maintenance level. The American College of Sports Medicine (ACSM) recommends that calorie levels never drop below 1,200 calories per day for women or 1,800 per day for men.

An alternative way to calculate a safe minimum calorie-intake level is to reduce calories by no more than 15 to 20 percent of your daily calorie maintenance needs.

Exercise is vital to lose weight. Physical activity improves muscle/fat ratio. It raises metabolism for easier weight loss and boosts motivation.

A Healthy Weight Loss Diet

If weight loss is the goal, the eating plan below is recommended by experts as being both safe and effective. Your daily diet should include:

- Between 1,200 and 2,200 calories a day, depending on your sex and how much weight you have to lose.

- About 25 to 30 percent calories from fat, of which no more than one-third should be saturated fat. Vegetable fats or fish oils are preferable to other animal fats.

- About 50 to 60 percent of calories should be from carbohydrates. Choose whole grains when possible.

- About 15 to 20 percent of calories from protein.

- A balanced variety of unprocessed fresh foods that keep your body healthy.

- A weight loss of no more than two to three pounds per week.

Watch out for weight loss gimmicks such as restrictions on certain foods or a specific combination of foods. These diets achieve weight loss by delivering a very low level of calories, not because of their gimmicky formulas. Also, choose a diet that focuses on real food, not food replacements or supplements.

The Importance of Exercise

The other half of the equation is physical exercise. Whether your goal is to lose or maintain weight, exercise is key. Although exercise may burn relatively few calories, a negative energy balance of as little as 200 calories a day can result in weight loss over time.

The Surgeon General of the United States recommends moderate activity of about 150 calories per day or 1,000 calories per week. Most experts suggest moderately intense aerobic activity should be performed most days of the week.

For best weight loss and long-term weight maintenance, you should combine cardio-aerobic exercise with weight/strength training. Walking, running, hiking, stair climbing, swimming, cycling, rowing, dancing, skating, cross-country skiing, and rope jumping are examples of cardio-aerobic exercise.

Weight training builds muscle mass to raise your metabolic rate. One pound of muscle can burn 30 to 50 calories a day, while one pound of fat burns only 3 calories a day.

Together, a healthy eating plan and regular physical activity are the best path to maintaining a healthy weight.

Information for the Student:
Nutrition, Exercise, and Metabolism

Our society is facing a crisis. More than one-fourth of students in the United States are over weight. Every year, more and more kids are becoming obese. Excess body weight can cause a wide range of health problems, from increasing the risk of diabetes and heart disease to increased rates of asthma and immune system disorders.

In an attempt to shed unwanted pounds, many people also go too far. Eating disorders such as anorexia and bulimia are increasingly common in people as young as 10 years old.

What is the best way to maintain a healthy body weight? In this unit you will explore how body fat is gained, stored, and used. You will learn about how diet and exercise work together to affect weight gain or loss. You will also learn how to evaluate popular diet plans for safety and effectiveness.

To succeed in this activity, you will need to do research using a variety of media and information sources. As you perform your research, keep in mind the following questions:

- Where are the best places to find the information I need? What types of materials will be the most useful?

- Is the source for my information reliable and accurate? Who is providing the information?

- Is the information relevant? How does this source help me answer the questions I am being asked or solve the problem I am being posed?

- How can I organize the information I find to make effective use of it when I need it?

- How can I effectively compare the claims of a diet plan to what I learn about safe and effective weight loss or maintenance techniques?

- Did I record the sources of information I used so that I can create a bibliography?

Keep all of your work on this project—notes, worksheets, and reference information— together in a file folder or binder.

Student Worksheet 4-1

Name _____ **Date** _____

Feast or Famine: Human Metabolism at Work

All people need energy from food to maintain body processes. How does food fuel our bodies? And how is excess fuel stored? What happens when we take in more food energy than we need? What happens when we do not take in enough?

Use at least **six** different sources to find out more about human metabolism. Choose at least **three** different types of sources, such as reference books, periodicals, Web sites, or encyclopedias.

Use the back of this sheet or your journal to take notes about the information that you find. Write down the name and bibliographic information for each source you use for future reference.

When you have completed your research, create a bibliography that lists all your sources in alphabetical order. Then answer the following questions:

- What is a calorie? _____

  _____

- What does the term *metabolism* mean? _____

  _____

- How is food energy stored in the body? _____

  _____

- How does your body make use of food energy to fuel body processes? _____

  _____

- What happens inside the body if there is an excess of food energy? _____

  _____

- What happens if there is a shortage of food energy? _____

  _____

- How does exercise affect the amount of energy needed by the body? _____

  _____

Student Worksheet 4-2

Name _____ **Date** _____

A Healthy Lifestyle

What is the best way to maintain a healthy body weight? Choose at least **three** different types of sources, such as reference books, periodicals, Web sites, or encyclopedias, to find the answer. Then complete the items below:

- The sources I used to find this information are:

_____

_____

- To maintain a healthy body weight, _____ intake must equal _____ expenditure.

- To lose weight, you must either _____ or

_____.

- Why are very low calorie diets unsafe?

_____

- Why are diets that limit types of foods unsafe?

_____

- Why is exercise an important part of any weight loss or weight maintenance program?

_____

- What do the letters BMI stand for? How is knowing your BMI helpful in assessing your weight?

_____

- What is one safe way to increase your metabolism?

_____

Student Worksheet 4-3

Name _____ **Date** _____

Diet Round-Up

For this activity, you will choose a popular diet regimen for study and evaluation.

Choose a popular plan that you have seen described in a book or a magazine article. Make a list of the claims made for the diet. Make sure to include the rules and procedures for the plan. Then compare the diet to what you know about safe and effective weight loss. Make a table to help organize your findings. Use the example below as a model for your own chart. Then answer the questions.

	A Healthy Diet	**This Diet: [Name]**
Limits certain types of foods	No	Yes
Includes exercise	Yes	No
Recommends no more than two pounds of weight loss per week	Yes	No

Do you think this diet is safe and effective? Why or why not?

_____

What is the best aspect of this diet?

_____

What is the worst aspect of this diet?

_____

What might happen to a person who follows this diet regimen for a month?

_____

What changes would you make to this diet to improve it?

_____

Would you recommend this diet to a friend? Why? Why not?

_____

Part 2—Healthy Habits at Home

Background Information for the Teacher and Library Media Specialist

In part 2 of this unit, students will apply what they have learned to do a scientific study of their own eating and exercise habits. This information will be kept in a personal journal and will not be shared with the class. Working together, the class will then prepare an information brochure with guidelines for safe and healthy eating and exercise habits for distribution to the school population.

Lesson Outline

Stimulate interest in this portion of the unit by asking students how their own eating and exercise habits compare to the best practices they have discovered. Explain to students that although they may have a rough idea of their calorie intake and expenditure, they will need to collect data for a more accurate assessment.

Explain to students that they will be conducting a scientific experiment using themselves as the research subjects. Reinforce for students that they will be working independently on this project and that no personal information will be shared with other members of the class.

Ask students how they will collect data for this experiment. Remind them that they will need to obtain information on both their daily calorie intake and their daily calorie expenditure. Where can they find this information? Jot down suggestions from the class on the blackboard.

Ask students how they will record the data from the experiment. What organizational tools will be most effective? Personal dairies, computer databases, or spreadsheets can all be effective tools.

Tell students that after they have completed their research, they will assess their habits. They will then devise a plan to achieve their personal health goals.

Ask students how they can create a workable plan and stick to it. What techniques can the class use to keep motivated? Develop a list of tips. Post it on the blackboard for reference.

Advise students that the final step in this project will be to create an information booklet that details the class's findings for distribution to the general school population. Ask students how they will coordinate the planning, writing, graphic design, production, and distribution of the booklet. Review the components of this project as necessary. Hand out Research Project Checklist 1 (Student Worksheet 1-A) to help students track their progress on this activity.

Information for the Student: Healthy Habits at Home

In part 1 of this activity, you researched human metabolism and healthy ways to maintain body weight.

In part 2 of this project, you will apply what you have learned to a study of your own health practices.

To succeed in this activity, you will work independently to collect and record data. You will assess your own eating and exercise habits. Then you will create a health maintenance plan for yourself. Finally, you will work with the other students in your class to communicate your findings on how to maintain a healthy lifestyle to the rest of your school. As you engage in your project, keep in mind the following questions:

- What information will I need for this project?

- Where are the best places to find the information I need? What types of materials will be the most useful?

- What organizational tools will best track the data and support my project?

- What materials will I need to conduct my experiment?

- How can I best contribute to the class project?

Student Worksheet 4-4

Name _____ Date _____

Calorie Intake and Expenditure Journal

Write down **everything** you eat for the duration of this unit. Also keep a record of all of your physical activity. Use the chart below to begin recording your data. Once you have completed this chart, use it as a model for recording further data in your science journal.

Date _____

CALORIE INTAKE:

Meal or Snack?	Time	Food	Quantity	Calories	Total

Total Meal: _____

Total Day Intake: _____

CALORIE EXPENDITURE:

Activity	Time	Duration	Calories/Minute	Total

Total day intake: **Total Day Expenditure:** _____

 - **Total Day Expenditure**

+/- _____

Student Worksheet 4-5

Name _____ Date _____

The Food Pyramid

Research the USDA recommendations for how many servings of each food type you should eat. Then fill in the food pyramid below with the appropriate data.

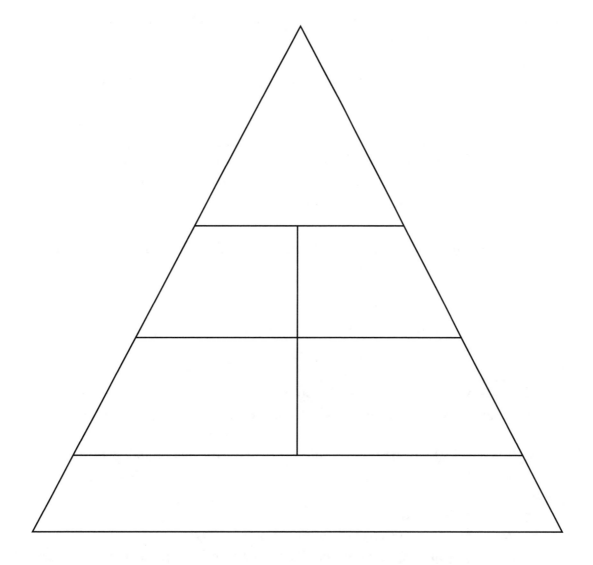

Student Worksheet 4-6

Name _____ **Date** _____

Healthy Habits at Home: Self-Assessment

Use the scoresheet below to assess your own health habits. Add up your total score.

Quality of Diet

   3   I eat a wide variety of nutritious foods from all food groups. I avoid fatty, highly processed, or sugary foods.

   2   I sometimes eat nutritious foods. I also sometimes eat fatty, sugary, or highly processed foods.

   1   I do not eat very many nutritious foods. I generally eat fast food and "junk" foods that are high in fats and sugar.

Calorie Intake

   3   I eat about the recommended number of calories needed per day for my age, weight, height and gender or have adjusted my daily calorie intake by a safe amount to meet my weight gain or loss goals.

   2   I eat somewhat more or less than the recommended number of calories needed per day for my age, weight, height and gender to maintain my weight or for safe weight loss or gain.

   1   I eat significantly more or less than the recommended number of calories needed per day for my age, weight, height and gender.

Calorie Expenditure

   3   I am very active and engage in sports or other physical pursuits 30 minutes or more per day, five to seven days per week.

   2   I am moderately active and engage in sports or other physical pursuits 30 minutes or more per day, three to five days per week.

   1   I am mostly sedentary and engage in sports or other physical pursuits less than three days per week.

BMI

   3   My Body Mass Index percentile is appropriate for my age and gender.

   2   My Body Mass Index percentile is at the low or high end of the healthy range for my age and gender.

   1   My Body Mass Index percentile indicates I am overweight or underweight for my age and gender.

Scoring:

       10–12:   **Great Going!**

         7–9:   **Not bad, but you can make improvements!**

         5–6:   **Try increasing your activity level and reducing the amount of junk food in your diet.**

           4:   **You should get more exercise and eat more low calorie, nutritious foods for optimum health and fitness.**

Student Worksheet 4-7

Name _____ **Date** _____

My Health Plan

Fill in the calendar below with healthy activities that you will plan to incorporate into your schedule. Consider a variety of sports. Don't forget to include chores such as walking the dog or washing dishes!

Then make a list of ways to improve your eating habits. Include Dos (e.g., DO eat five to seven servings of fruit and vegetables a day) as well as Don'ts (DON'T snack on high-fat treats while watching TV).

Place your goal sheet in a prominent place at home to help you maintain a healthy lifestyle.

Month: _____

Sunday	Monday	Tuesday	Wednesday	Thursday	Friday	Saturday

Student Worksheet 4-8

Name _____ **Date** _____

A Guide to Healthy Living

For this activity, you will collaborate with the other students in your class to create an information booklet. The booklet will contain guidelines for how to maintain a healthy weight through proper diet and exercise.

To create the booklet, decide who will be responsible for each of the following areas:

- Planning the content of the brochure

  _____

- Writing the text for the brochure

  _____

- Fact-checking the brochure

  _____

- Creating the graphic elements for the brochure

  _____

- Producing the brochure

  _____

- Distributing the brochure

  _____

Make sure the completed brochure contains the following elements:

- A title;
- A masthead (a list of the people who produced the brochure, and their contributions);
- Correct and complete citations for all sources of material, including illustrations;
- A list of additional resources for students to consult if they want more information; and
- Verifiable facts.

Organizational and Assessment Checklist for the Teacher

Lesson Component	Taught/Assessed by	Assessment Method
Introducing the Lesson —General Introduction • Identifying sources • How to prepare a bibliography		
Feast or Famine: Human Metabolism at Work		• Review Worksheet 4-1 answers for student comprehension of the material
A Healthy Lifestyle		• Review Worksheet 4-2 answers for student comprehension of the material
Diet Round-Up		• Review Worksheet 4-3 answers for student comprehension of the material
Introduction to Part 2		
Calorie Intake and Expenditure Journal		• Review journal for completeness
The Food Pyramid		• Review Worksheet 4-5 answers for student comprehension of the material
Healthy Habits at Home: Self-Assessment		• Review Worksheet 4-6 answers for student comprehension of the material
My Health Plan		• Review student calendar for completeness and quality of items included
A Guide to Healthy Living • Supervise assignment of tasks for fairness and participation of all • Direct creation of text and artwork • Direct production of booklet • Direct distribution of booklet		• Review booklet for completeness.

Selected Suggested Resources/Bibliography

Items marked with an asterisk would be suitable for teacher background; all others would be for both teacher and student reference.

Web Sites

http://kidshealth.org/teen/food_fitness/dieting/bmi.html ©1995-2004 The Nemours Foundation.
Health resource for teens pitched at an easy-to-understand level, with nice graphics and solid information. Includes charts for plotting BMI for age.

http://147.208.9.133/Default.asp
The Interactive Healthy Eating Index. U.S. government Web site provides data and software for recording calories consumed and computing physical activity calorie expenditures.

www.caloriecontrol.org/
The Calorie Control Council gives good advice on cutting calories and maintaining a healthy weight. Online calorie counter.

www.nutritiondata.com/
Online calorie counter and calculator.

www.caloriesperhour.com/
Calorie counter and calculator for calories burned, food, fast food, low carb, BMI, BMR, RMR, and weight loss; diet and weight loss tips and weight loss program.

www.primusweb.com/fitnesspartner/jumpsite/calculat.htm
Calorie expenditure calculator based on the Compendium of Physical Activity.

www.caloriecountercharts.com/
Mike's Calorie and Fat Gram Chart for 1000 Foods. Won an award from *The Los Angeles Times* for value to their readership.

www.caloriecountercharts.com/chart1a.htm
Calorie and fat gram charts sorted alphabetically.

www.stevenscreek.com/goodies/calories.shtml
Calorie calculator. A service of Stevens Creek Software.

www.calorie-count.com
Calorie counter with nutritional data for thousands of foods.

www.barc.usda.gov/bhnrc
Beltsville Human Nutrition Research Center (BHNRC)—Defines, through research, the role of food and its components in optimizing human health and reducing the risk of nutritionally related disorders in the diverse population (Department of Agriculture [USDA], Agriculture Research Service (ARS); Beltsville Agricultural Research Center [BARC]).

www.nal.usda.gov/fnic/etext/000023.html
This Food and Nutrition Information Center (FNIC) topic page was designed to provide information on food guide pyramids for different types of ethnic and cultural groups.

kidshealth.org/parent/nutrition_fit/ nutrition/pyramid.html
Advice on how to use the food guide to create healthy meals for children.

www.usda.gov/news/usdakids/food_pyr.html
   Food pyramid information for kids.

www.ring.com/health/food/food.htm
   Instructions on how to use the food pyramid.

www.bcm.edu/cnrc/
   Children's Nutrition Research Center at Baylor College of Medicine (CNRC) is dedicated to defining the nutrient needs of children, from conception through adolescence. Good source for reliable information.

www.fda.gov/oc/opacom/kids/
   FDA Kids Home Page—(Department of Health and Human Services (HHS), Food and Drug Administration [FDA]). Very useful government source aimed at a younger audience. Lots of health information.

www.nal.usda.gov/fnic/Fpyr/pyramid.html
   This Food and Nutrition Information Center (FNIC) topic page was designed to provide information on the Food Guide Pyramid. (FNIC) is located at the National Agricultural Library (NAL) and is part of the U.S. Department of Agriculture (USDA).

www.usda.gov/cnpp/healthyeating.html
   USDA Healthy Eating Index is a summary measure of overall diet quality. Includes *Interactive Healthy Eating Index*, an online dietary assessment tool with nutrition messages and links.

www.health.gov/dietaryguidelines/
   Nutrition and Your Health: Dietary Guidelines for Americans—Guidelines for fitness and nutrition. (Department of Health and Human Services [HHS]).

www.Nutrition.gov
   Provides easy access to all online federal government information on nutrition (multiple agencies involved).

http://www.bcm.tmc.edu/cnrc/consumer/nyc/vol1_03/energy_calculator.htm
   Energy needs calculator for kids.

http://www.bcm.tmc.edu/cnrc/consumer/archives/hype_hope.htm
   Guidelines for evaluating diet advice.

Print Resources

American College of Sports Medicine, *Principles of Exercise Prescription*. Philadelphia: William & Wilkins, 1995.

Hammer, L. D., H. C. Kraemer, D. M. Wilson, P. L. Ritter, and S M. Dornbusch. "Standardized Percentile Curves of Body-Mass Index for Children and Adolescents." *American Journal of Disease of Child* 145 (1991): 259–263.

*Lowry, R., et al. "Weight Management Goals & Practices Among U.S. High School Students: Associations with Physical Activity, Diet, and Smoking." *Journal of Adolescent Health* 31 (2002): 133–144.

*Pietrobelli, A., M. S. Faith, D. B. Allison, D. Gallagher, G. Chiumello, and S. B. Heymsfield. "Body Mass Index as a Measure of Adiposity among Children and Adolescents: A Validation Study." *Journal of Pediatrics* 132 (1998): 204–210.

Sonberg, Lynn. *The Quick and Easy Fat Gram & Calorie Counter*. New York: Avon Books, 1992.

5

What Causes Milk to Spoil?:
Microorganisms at Work

Object of This Lesson

In this unit, students use library resources and a variety of research tools to learn about germ theory and its roots in groundbreaking work by Louis Pasteur and other 19th-century scientists. They will learn through an examination of information resources and hands-on investigation how microorganisms affect materials such as food and water, and how they can cause disease. They will perform lab activities involving growing microorganisms such as bacteria and molds.

Students will then discover the role of microorganisms in making and preserving food. They will research the history of bread, wine, pickles, or yogurt. They will then apply what they have learned to kitchen activities such as bread baking, pickle making, or yogurt making. Students will conclude the activity by creating a book of "Pasteur's Recipes."

This unit will support the following American Association for the Advancement of Science Benchmarks (p. 145):

- To determine that microorganisms are responsible for the processes of decay.

- To recognize that Louis Pasteur advanced the ideas behind the modern understanding of germ theory.

- To identify different types of microorganisms, such as bacteria, viruses, yeasts, and molds.

- To show that spoilage and fermentation occur when bacteria enter materials such as juice or milk, then reproduce and make waste products.

- To show that spoilage can be avoided by keeping germs out or by destroying them with heat.

- To understand that vaccines help the body produce immunity to some microorganisms.

- To recognize that germ theory changed health practices.

- To recognize the role of serendipity and accidents in scientific discovery.

- To understand the purposes of current health approaches and practices such as pasteurization, sanitation, and aseptic surgery.

- To recognize the purpose and function of microscopes and their role in the history of germ theory.

Science Content Knowledge and Skills

Students will

- Define the terms *microorganism, bacteria, virus, mold, yeast, vaccine,* and *pasteurization*;

- Describe, verbally and in writing, how bacteria cause spoilage and fermentation;

- Describe the findings of Louis Pasteur and how they affect modern health practices;

- Define and explain the expression "germ theory";

- Describe how specific germs cause specific diseases;

- Describe how vaccines help in the prevention of disease and by what process;

- Explain how microorganisms are used to make wine, bread, pickles, cheese, and yogurt;

- Use a microscope; and

- Conduct a lab experiment and write a lab report.

Information Literacy Knowledge and Skills

Students will

- Use a variety of different index types to locate material;

- Use periodicals, popular science and health guides, government resources, and scientific documents to collect information;

- Describe how they found and chose their resources;

- Evaluate the appropriateness of the research material;

- Judge and support judgments of the degree of inaccuracy, bias, or misleading information in information sources;

- Identify three different types of media used to find the information required;

- Prepare a complete bibliography;

- Present information in a clear and organized manner;

- Express information creatively and evaluate strengths and weaknesses of creative presentations of information;

- Apply knowledge and integrate it with new information to create new meaning; and

- Work with others, in person and through remote technologies, to create and evaluate complex information products that integrate information in a variety of formats.

Lesson Outline

This lesson is designed to be team-taught by a library media specialist and a science specialist. Before you introduce the lesson to students, decide which aspects of the unit will be presented by each member of the team. Decide who will assess student performance on each component of the unit. Use the checklist at the end of this chapter to assist you in organizing these aspects of teaching this unit.

Stimulate interest in the lesson by asking students if they have ever eaten cheese or yogurt. Ask them: Did you know you are eating mold and bacteria waste products when you consume these foods? Ask students if they know the origin and meaning of the term *pasteurization*.

Explain to students that you will be leading a research project into microorganisms and the scientific development of germ theory. They will learn about the experiments and discoveries of Louis Pasteur and other pioneers in the field of microbiology. Explain that the students will be conducting research by consulting many different types of sources. Ask students where they might find information on this topic. Create a list of possible sources of information on the blackboard.

Ask students how they will organize the information they collect. Brainstorm methods and materials to help in the organization and retrieval of data for this project. Reinforce the concept of the bibliography. How will a bibliography help students keep track of their data? How will preparing the bibliography properly safeguard against misleading information? How else will a bibliography be useful?

Go over the proper format of bibliographical entries for different types of resources. Make sure students know which information is important for the bibliography and which information is not required. Also show students where the necessary information can be located, for example, in the front of a book or at the bottom of a Web page.

Explain to students that, after they have completed their research, they will culture their own mold and bacteria in a variety of lab experiments and activities. They will use a microscope to study examples of microorganisms and write up lab reports of their findings.

Ask students if they have any questions about how to proceed with the first step of the project. Review as needed. It may be helpful to list all the steps required for completion of this project on the blackboard. Encourage students to use Research Project Checklist 1 (Student Worksheet 1-A) as a model for their own checklists.

Part 1—What Causes Milk to Spoil?: Microorganisms at Work

Background Information for the Teacher and Library Media Specialist

Microbes are everywhere. They are the oldest forms of life on Earth. Microbe fossils date back more than 3.5 billion years. But what exactly is a microbe?

Types of Microbes

There are five main types of microbes. *Archaea* resemble bacteria and give clues about the earliest forms of life on Earth. They thrive in extreme environments such as geyser shelves and hot pools.

Bacteria are the largest group of microbes. There are thousands of different types. They can be classified according to their cell shapes: Spherical (coccus), Short Plump Rod (cocco-bacillus), Rod-shaped (bacillus), Spiral (spirillum), and Comma-shaped (vibrio). They also vary in size and their requirements for oxygen.

Bacteria reproduce rapidly by the process of binary fission. They can reproduce every 20 minutes in conducive conditions.

Only a few types of bacteria are harmful or deadly. These, however, can have far-reaching consequences. They cause some types of food poisoning, such as botulism. They can cause diseases such as strep throat, pneumonia, tuberculosis, or cholera.

Many types of bacteria, however, are helpful. They help digest food in our intestines and produce vitamins our bodies need to survive. Bacteria colonies on our skin protect us from infection from less amenable microbes. Bacteria also are effective in making and preserving some foods, such as yogurt, and materials such as leather.

Fungi are a third type of microbe. They can range from single-celled yeast to a 3.5-mile-wide mushroom. Fungi decompose waste and are crucial in the manufacture of bread, wine, and beer through the process of fermentation.

Protista are another type of microorganism. They can be plant-like or animal-like, or a combination of the two. Amoebae and euglenae are examples of protista.

Viruses are the fifth category of microbe. Many scientists disagree about whether viruses are actually living things, as they cannot reproduce or engage in any life processes on their own. They must enter into host cells to reproduce. There, they frequently wreak havoc and cause disease.

There are over 4,000 known viruses. Of these, only about 250 viruses can infect humans. Most viruses are 20 to 100 times smaller than bacteria and are too small to be seen through a light microscope.

History of Microbiology

The story of microbes began when the Dutch naturalist, Anton van Leeuwenhoek, became the first to see single-celled life forms swimming around in blood, sperm, and pond water. He called these organisms "animalcules."

As microscopes improved, it was possible to see more and more "animalcules" in various substances. But what they were, and what role they played in life systems and chemical reactions, was not understood until the 19th century.

Louis Pasteur

Louis Pasteur was born in 1822, the only son of a poorly educated tanner. The headmaster of the local college convinced father and son that Louis should apply to the Ecole Normale Superieure in Paris, a prestigious French university. Pasteur thus began his long career as a chemist, studying the shapes of organic crystals.

In 1854 he was appointed dean and professor of chemistry at the Faculty of Sciences in Lille, France. Lille was an industrial town with many distilleries and factories. When the manager of one distillery approached him with a problem, he quickly solved the mystery of what caused alcoholic fermentation. He concluded that living cells were responsible for forming alcohol from sugar, and that contamination by other microorganisms interfered with the process.

Pasteur identified and isolated the microorganisms responsible for fermenting wine, beer, and vinegar. He also showed that if he heated wine, beer, or milk for a few minutes, he could kill microorganisms and thereby prevent spoilage. This process, known as pasteurization, is still used today.

Based on his work on fermentation, it seemed obvious to Pasteur that yeasts and other microorganisms entered from the outside, for example, on the dust of the air. Pasteur conducted a series of clever experiments that conclusively destroyed any argument for "spontaneous generation," the then-current theory of life's origins.

The highlights of Pasteur's career were the development of the germ theory of disease and the subsequent use of vaccination as a method to prevent disease. Joseph Lister was particularly impressed by Pasteur's research. He instituted the systematic sterilization of instruments and bandages in hospitals and began spraying phenol solutions in his own operating rooms before surgery. These practices reduced the incidence of infections after surgery to unprecedented low numbers.

By 1875 many other physicians began to accept Pasteur's germ theory in principle. Yet the establishment was still not ready to concede that major diseases such as cholera, diphtheria, scarlet fever, puerperal fever, or smallpox were caused by germs. Nor were they willing to concede that their own actions and behavior might be causing infection.

Pasteur realized that infection was commonly spread by physicians and hospital attendants as they moved between sick and healthy patients. In an impassioned speech, he urged physicians to avoid microbes as a means to prevent infection. "This water, this sponge, this lint with which you wash or cover a wound, may deposit germs which have the power of multiplying rapidly within the tissue. . . . If I had the honor of being a surgeon . . . not only would I use none but perfectly clean instruments, but I would clean my hands with the greatest care."

Slowly but surely Pasteur's message caught on. Antiseptic practices in medicine and surgery became the rule.

Development of Vaccines

In 1796, Edward Jenner, a country doctor, noticed that milkmaids who contracted cowpox became immune to the more serious disease of smallpox. He began experimenting with fluid from fresh cowpox sores. He used it to inoculate an eight-year-old boy. The experiment was a success. By 1800, more than 100,000 people had been vaccinated against smallpox using Jenner's method.

Louis Pasteur was studying anthrax when he accidentally inoculated some chickens with bacteria. He realized he had inadvertently duplicated Jenner's experiments. So began the modern history of inoculation.

Pasteur then went on to develop a vaccine for rabies. Also known as hydrophobia, rabies was widely feared as a terrible disease that caused an excruciatingly painful death. There had never been a cure for rabies. It was always fatal.

On July 6, 1885, nine-year-old Joseph Meister and his mother came to Pasteur's laboratory. Joseph had been bitten by a rabid dog. Pasteur treated him with his preliminary vaccine. Joseph made a perfect recovery.

When news of the successful vaccination was made public, Louis Pasteur became a hero. But it was the last accomplishment of his productive life. He suffered a stroke at age 46 and died in 1895.

Information for the Student: Microorganisms at Work

Until the 19th century, people really did not know what caused most diseases. Germs were completely unknown. Because they are so small, no one had ever seen a bacterium or virus.

The microscope made microorganisms visible for the first time. Scientists such as Louis Pasteur built on what they learned via the microscope to revolutionize science and medicine. The germ theory of disease grew out of Pasteur's observations and discoveries.

In this unit, you will explore microorganisms such as molds, viruses, and bacteria. You will learn about how they can cause disease. You will also learn how they serve important roles in making and preserving food. You will also have the opportunity to grow microorganisms on your own and observe them under a microscope.

To succeed in this activity, you will need to do research using a variety of media and information sources. As you perform your research, keep in mind the following questions:

- Where are the best places to find the information I need? What types of materials will be the most useful?

- Is the source for my information reliable and accurate? Who is providing the information?

- Is the information relevant? How does this source help me answer the questions I am being asked or solve the problem I am being posed?

- How can I organize the information I find to make effective use of it when I need it?

- Did I record the sources of information I used so that I can create a bibliography?

- Did I collect all the information I need to conduct an experiment of my own?

Keep all of your work on this project—notes, worksheets, and reference information—together in a file folder or binder.

Student Worksheet 5-1

Name _____ Date _____

Louis Pasteur and Germ Theory

Louis Pasteur was the leading biologist of the 19th century. His discoveries changed the way we view the world.

Use at least **six** different sources to find out more about the discoveries of Louis Pasteur. Choose at least **three** different types of sources, such as reference books, periodicals, Web sites or encyclopedias. Use at least **one** primary source.

Use the back of this sheet or your journal to take notes about the information that you find. Write down the bibliographic information for each source you use for future reference.

When you have completed your research, create a bibliography that lists all of your sources in alphabetical order. Then answer the following questions:

- What was Louis Pasteur's first scientific discovery?

  _____

  _____

- Describe the meaning of the phrase "spontaneous generation," and how Pasteur disproved it.

  _____

  _____

- What is pasteurization?

  _____

  _____

- Describe how Pasteur accidentally developed a vaccine.

  _____

  _____

- Who was Joseph Meister, and how did Louis Pasteur help him?

  _____

  _____

Student Worksheet 5-2

Name _____ Date _____

Microbe Mania

What kinds of microbes are there? How are they alike? How do they differ?

Choose at least **three** different types of sources, such as reference books, periodicals, Web sites, or encyclopedias.

Use the back of this sheet or your journal to take notes about the information that you find. Write down the bibliographic information for each source you use for future reference.

When you have completed your research, create a bibliography that lists all of your sources in alphabetical order. Then answer the following questions:

- What is the most common type of microbe?

  _____

- What type of microbes may contain chlorophyll?

  _____

- How do viruses and bacteria compare in size?

  _____

- List three diseases caused by bacteria. List three diseases caused by viruses.

  _____

  _____

- Describe five ways microbes are helpful or necessary to humans.

  _____

- What causes milk to spoil?

  _____

Student Worksheet 5-3

Name _____ **Date** _____

Growing Bacteria Lab

Materials:

2 test tubes with screw cap	glass beaker
1 ml pipette	fat-free chicken or beef broth
10 ml pipette	1 mushroom
2 transfer pipettes	filter paper
2 test tubes with cap	saucepan

Procedure:

1. Chop the mushroom.
2. Put it into a saucepan (or in the beaker, in the microwave) with the broth. Bring to a boil.
3. Let cool to room temperature.
4. Pour the broth through the filter. The broth you use should be clear.
5. Use a transfer pipette to collect samples of bacteria. You may collect the samples from doorknobs, sink surfaces, or the inside of your mouth.
6. Pipette 10 ml of filtered broth and 2 ml of the "bacteria" sample in a test tube. Close the cap.
7. Place the tube in an incubator or other warm place. Repeat with a separate test tube for each bacteria sample.
8. Allow the samples to sit undisturbed for three days. Observe any changes in appearance. If bacteria are present, the sample will start to smell unpleasant and grow cloudy.

Answer the following questions:

• Did bacteria grow in your sample?

_____

• If you did not have a successful experiment, describe some reasons why it may have failed.

_____

• If your experiment was successful, describe the appearance of the sample after three days.

_____

• How many bacteria do you think might be in the test tube after three days? Explain your answer .

_____

Student Worksheet 5-4

Name _____ Date _____

Growing Mold Lab

Materials:
4 slices of bread
water
plastic wrap (or other airtight covering)
spray bottle

Procedure:

1. Cut one piece of bread in half. Seal one-half in plastic wrap. Expose the other to air.

2. Cut another piece of bread in half. Leave one-half in a dark place, such as a paper bag. Place the other half in strong light, such as direct sunlight.

3. Cut the third piece of bread in half. Keep one-half very dry. Sprinkle approximately 1 teaspoon of water on the other half. Using the spray bottle, add a few drops of water to this slice every day.

4. Cut the fourth piece of bread in half. Place one-half somewhere warm and dark. Place the second half somewhere cold and dark, such as in the refrigerator.

5. Examine the samples each day.

Answer the following questions:

• Where did mold grow most quickly?

_____

• Where did mold grow the least or not at all?

_____

• Do all the mold samples look the same? Describe.

_____

• What factors are important to mold growth?

_____

Student Worksheet 5-5

Name _____ **Date** _____

Microbes under the Microscope

Obtain a microbe sample from your own lab work or from your teacher. Examine the sample under the microscope. Then answer the questions below.

- What type of microbe is this?

  _____

- What distinguishing characteristics does this microbe have?

  _____

- How big is this microbe?

  _____

- At what power of magnification can you see this microbe best?

  _____

- Are you using any stains or special techniques to help you observe your sample? If so, list them here:

  _____

Draw what you see in your slide below. Make sure to use scale measurements and accurate, descriptive labels for your drawing. Use color to make your illustration more attractive and easier to understand.

Part 2—Microbes in the Kitchen

Background Information for the Teacher and Library Media Specialist

In part 1 of this activity, students researched microbes and the history of germ theory.

In part 2 of this project, they will learn more about how microbes help humans in the production and preservation of various types of food. They will engage in a lab activity in which they make types of foods that take advantage of microbes. They will then collaborate with other students in the class to produce a class "Microbe Cookbook."

Lesson Outline

Stimulate interest in this portion of the unit by asking students how the principles discovered by Pasteur and others have contributed to modern food science. Explain to students that they will be conducting scientific experiments in the kitchen using recipes for common foods for their materials and procedures.

Ask students how they will proceed with this experiment. Where can they find their information? Jot down suggestions from the class on the blackboard.

Ask students how they will record the data from the activity. What organizational tools will be most effective?

Tell students that after they have completed their research, they will compile a "Microbe Cookbook." Ask students how they will coordinate the planning, writing, graphic design, production, and distribution of the book. Review the components of this project as necessary. Use Research Project Checklist 1 (Student Worksheet 1-A) as a model for students to create their own checklists to track their progress on this activity.

Information for the Student: Microbes in the Kitchen

In part 1 of this activity, you researched microbes and the history of germ theory.

In part 2 of this project, you will learn more about how microbes help humans in the production and preservation of various types of food.

To succeed in this activity, you will work independently to collect and record data. Then you will engage in a "lab" activity in which you will make a type of food that takes advantage of microbes. Finally, you will collaborate with the other students in your class to communicate your findings by producing a class "Microbe Cookbook." As you engage in your project, keep in mind the following questions:

- What information will I need for this project?

- Where are the best places to find the information I need? What types of materials will be the most useful?

- What organizational tools will best track the data and support my project?

- What materials will I need to conduct my lab activity at home?

- How can I best contribute to the class project?

Student Worksheet 5-6

Name _____ **Date** _____

Microbes at Work in the Kitchen

Research the following foods. Find out how microbes are used to make them. Write a paragraph that describes your findings about each type of food.

Bread

Cheese

Yogurt

Vinegar

Soy sauce

Tea

Pickles

Student Worksheet 5-7

Name _____ Date _____

Microbes Cook!

Bread
Cheese
Yogurt
Vinegar
Soy sauce
Tea
Pickles

Find a recipe for one of the foods on the above list. Prepare the food at home. Then answer the following questions:

• Where did you find your recipe? _____

• Was the recipe easy to follow? _____

• What ingredients did you need? Did you have everything on hand at home?

   _____

• How long did it take to make this recipe? _____

• What microbe helped you make this recipe? _____

• What was the most interesting or fun part of making this recipe?

   _____

• How did the finished product taste? _____

• Would you serve this recipe to your classmates? _____

• Did your recipe "work?" Why or why not? _____

   _____

• What changes would you make to this recipe if you were to make it again?

   _____

The recipe will be collected into a cookbook called "Microbe Cookbook." Write or type a neat copy of your recipe. Design a cover for the cookbook. Hand in your recipe and cover along with this worksheet to your teacher.

Organizational and Assessment Checklist for the Teacher

Lesson Component	Taught/Assessed by	Assessment Method
Introducing the Lesson —General Introduction • Identifying sources • How to prepare a bibliography		
Louis Pasteur and Germ Theory		• Review Worksheet 5-1 answers for student comprehension of the material • Review bibliography for completeness and suitability of sources
Microbe Mania		• Review Worksheet 5-2 answers for student comprehension of the material • Review bibliography for completeness and suitability of sources
Growing Bacteria Lab • Supervise lab activity		• Review Worksheet 5-3 answers for student comprehension of the material
Growing Mold Lab • Supervise lab activity		• Review Worksheet 5-4 answers for student comprehension of the material
Microbes under the Microscope • Supervise lab activity		• Review Worksheet 5-5 answers for student comprehension of the material
Introduction to Part 2		
Microbes at Work in the Kitchen		• Review Worksheet 5-6 answers for student comprehension of the material
Microbes Cook! • Supervise assignment of tasks for cookbook • Direct preparation of text and artwork • Direct production of booklet • Direct distribution of booklet		• Review Worksheet 5-7 answers for student comprehension of the material

Selected Suggested Resources/Bibliography

Items marked with an asterisk would be suitable for teacher background; all others would be for both teacher and student reference.

Laboratory Materials

All of the materials suggested for this unit are readily available from any school supplier with a science focus. Live microbes can be obtained in either freeze-dried form or prepared as slants in culture tubes. Prepared slides of various types of bacteria and fungi are also readily available.

For a good assortment at reasonable prices, we recommend Nasco Scientific., 901 Janesville Ave., PO Box 901, Ft. Atkinson, WI 53558-0901, 800-558-9595.

Web Sites

ambafrance-ca.org/HYPERLAB/PEOPLE/_pasteur.html
    Biographical information on Louis Pasteur.

www.accessexcellence.org/AB/BC/Louis_Pasteur.html
    Biographical information on Louis Pasteur.

www.louisville.edu/library/ ekstrom/special/pasteur/cohn.html
    Includes *The Life and Times of Louis Pasteur,* a lecture by David V. Cohn.

www.labexplorer.com/louis_pasteur.htm
    Biography plus links to other materials on Pasteur.

www.panspermia.org/pasteur.htm
    Biography plus links to other materials on Pasteur.

scienceworld.wolfram.com/biography/Pasteur.html
    Brief biography of Pasteur.

* http://www.kidzone.ws/science/mold.htm
    Grow mold experiment.

* http://www.brightminds.uq.edu.au/thelab/fermentation/what_to_do.html
    Fermentation experiment using yeast.

*http://www.healthyhands.com/educator/grades_3_6/lesson_1_1.htm
    Lesson suggestions and reproducible worksheets for a microbe activity.

http://www.microbeworld.org/htm/aboutmicro/abt_start.htm
    American Society for Microbiology. Good discussion of various types of microbes.

www.actionbioscience.org/
    ActionBioScience is a Web-based educational resource produced by the American Institute of Biological Sciences to raise scientific literacy. Among the topics the site covers are microbiology, microbial forensics, and antibiotic resistance.

www.biology-online.org/
   Biology Online is an educational site that includes information on genetics, microscopy, microbiology, and more from Pennsylvania State University's biological science course.

helios.bto.ed.ac.uk/bto/microbes
   Extensive educational resource about microorganisms from the University of Edinburgh.

http://www.bact.wisc.edu/resources/GenInfo.html
   The University of Wisconsin's Information about Microbiology for the Public has links to science news, other microbiology sites, and an online microbiology textbook that provides detailed information on microbes.

http://www.ici.com/ici_schools/pages/resources/yeast.htm—
   Educational site from the United Kingdom covers everything you ever wanted to know about yeast.

http://commtechlab.msu.edu/sites/dlc-me/zoo/zbmain.html
   The Microbe Snack Bar—information on how different microorganisms make food.

* http://www.sasked.gov.sk.ca/docs/midlsci/gr7ufmsc.html
   Microrganism unit for grade 7 students from Saskatchewan Ministry of Education, Canada.

www.healingcrow.com/ferfun/ferfun.html
   Nonprofit corporation provides recipes for fermented foods, including yogurt and sauerkraut.

http://www.bact.wisc.edu/bact303/b1
   Life at High Temperatures focuses on the amazing bacteria that thrive in Yellowstone National Park's hot springs and geysers.

http://www.ucmp.berkeley.edu/archaea/archaea.html
   The University of California, Berkeley, provides an introduction to the Archaea.

6

The Disappearing Rainforest: The Effects of Human Action on the Environment

Object of This Lesson

In this unit, students will use library resources and a variety of research tools to learn about the tropical rainforest ecosystem. They will learn about the diversity of life supported by the ecosystem and about how the entire system is joined together into a self-supporting web.

Students will then learn how human activities are affecting the ecosystem, and how its damage in turn affects the ability of the planet to sustain life. They will perform a lab activity that demonstrates the greenhouse effect. They will then prepare reports detailing the causes of deforestation. Students will conclude the activity by creating a PowerPoint presentation that offers a program for rainforest renewal.

This unit will support the following American Association for the Advancement of Science Benchmarks (p. 73, p. 104, p. 117, p. 155, p. 177):

- To determine that human activities, such as reducing the amount of forest cover, have changed the earth's land, oceans, and atmosphere.

- To recognize that some of these changes have decreased the capacity of the environment to support some life forms.

- To recognize that all organisms, including the human species, are part of and depend on interconnected global food webs.

- To illustrate that human beings are part of the earth's ecosystems, and that human activities can deliberately or inadvertently alter the equilibrium in ecosystems.

- To understand that new technology can change cultural values and social behavior.

- To recognize that the global environment is affected by national policies and practices relating to energy use, waste disposal, ecological management, manufacturing, and population.

- To simulate the planning and use of available resources for the greatest benefit.

- To make choices about what, how much, and how to produce things to meet wants and needs of various communities.

- To trace and understand how policies of market participants or government agencies affect the production and distribution of resources.

Science Content Knowledge and Skills

Students will

- Define the terms *ecosystem, rainforest, interdependence*, and *biome*;

- Describe, verbally and in writing, the life cycles of some of the plants and animals that live in tropical rainforest regions;

- Identify major rainforest ecosystems of Africa, Asia, South America, Australia, and North/Central America;

- Describe the physical structure of a typical rainforest;

- Describe how plants in a rainforest compete for scarce resources;

- Describe how the rainforest is important to Earth as a whole, for example, as a producer of oxygen;

- Describe and explain the meaning of the phrase "the greenhouse effect" and its relationship to the rainforest;

- Conduct a lab experiment and write a lab report; and

- Describe several human activities, such as mining, agriculture, and logging, that are causes of deforestation.

Information Literacy Knowledge and Skills

Students will

- Use a variety of different index types to locate material;

- Use periodicals, reference books, Web sites, government resources and scientific documents to collect information;

- Describe how they found and chose their resources;

- Evaluate the appropriateness of the research material;

- Judge and support judgments of the degree of inaccuracy, bias, or misleading information in information sources;

- Identify three different types of media used to find the information required;

- Prepare a complete bibliography;

- Present information in a clear and organized manner;

- Express information creatively and evaluate strengths and weaknesses of creative presentations of information;

- Apply knowledge and integrate it new information to create new meaning;

- Connect to larger ideas in the human experience and their own lives;

- Use maps to find patterns of change over time;

- Work with others, in person and through remote technologies, to create and evaluate complex information products that integrate information in a variety of formats; and

- Use desktop publishing software to create a variety of products and publications.

Lesson Outline

This lesson is designed to be team-taught by a library media specialist and a science specialist. Before you introduce the lesson to students, decide which aspects of the unit will be presented by each member of the team. Decide who will assess student performance on each component of the unit. Use the checklist at the end of this chapter to assist you in organizing these aspects of teaching the unit.

Stimulate interest in the lesson by asking students by asking students to describe what they know about rainforests. Have students identify regions where rainforests can be found on a world map.

Explain to students that you will be leading a research project into the rainforest ecosystem and how it is changing. Say that they will learn about the plants, animals, and people who live in the rainforests and about how the actions of humans are causing the rainforest to disappear. Explain that the students will be conducting research by consulting many different types of sources. Ask students where they might find information on this topic. Create a list of possible sources of information on the blackboard.

Ask students how they will organize the information they collect. Brainstorm methods and materials to help in the organization and retrieval of data for this project. Introduce the concept of the bibliography. How will a bibliography help students keep track of their data? How will preparing the bibliography properly safeguard against misleading information? How else will a bibliography be useful?

Go over the proper format of bibliographical entries for different types of resources. Make sure students know which information is important for the bibliography and which information is not required. Also show students where the necessary information can be located, for example, in the front of a book or at the bottom of a Web page.

Explain to students that, after they have completed their initial research, they will prepare four-story dioramas to present detailed, three-dimensional portraits of various rainforest ecosystems.

Ask students if they have any questions about how to proceed with the first step of the project. Review as needed. It may be helpful to list all the steps required for completion of this project on the blackboard. Encourage students to use Research Project Checklist 1 (Student Worksheet 1-A) to keep track of their work in their journal.

Part 1—The Effects of Human Action on the Environment

Background Information for the Teacher and Library Media Specialist

Rainforests are the emerald jewels that glitter atop the earthly crown. They have evolved over millions of years into complex environments that support an incredible diversity of life. More than one-third of all forms of life on Earth dwell in the rainforest—30 million different types of insects alone!

Characteristics of the Rainforest

Rainforests are characterized by warm average temperatures (68–930° F/20–340° C) and by plenty of rainfall (60–400 inches/152–1016 cm). Rain falls nearly every day.

Within the rainforest habitat, there are several discrete zones, or strata. At the base of the system is the forest floor. Little light reaches it, and the soil is thin and poor.

Although the forest floor does not support much plant life, it is teeming with animal life. Insects and arachnids abound. Termites, for example, build nests the size of soccer balls, and travel back and forth from them by way of long, winding tunnels built on tree trunks. Dozens of ant species also live on the forest floor.

Reptiles also thrive here. Since they cannot regulate their own body temperature, they must depend on environmental conditions to keep them warm. The heat and humidity of the rainforest floor are perfect for sustaining lizards and snakes such as the Fer-de-lance or Anaconda.

Above the forest floor is the dark, shady area known as the understory. Very little sunlight ever reaches here—less than 5 percent of the sun's energy. Most plants in the understory have adapted to low, filtered light and poor soil. Leaves are often very large to make the best use of any available sunlight. Plants here grow very slowly. Some, such as bromeliads, rely on wind to spread their pollen and seeds.

Above the understory is the rainforest canopy. It is the ceiling of the rainforest. Many rainforest birds, such as parrots and toucans, are year-round residents. Others, such as flycatchers or warblers, migrate to rainforests in the winter from more northern climes.

More than half of the rainforest's mammals live in the canopy. Many species of animals live out their entire lives here without ever touching the ground.

Above the canopy is the rainforest's emergent layer. It is composed of scattered, super-tall trees, most of which reach over 130 feet/40 meters. These trees tend to be very straight, with just a few lower branches.

Eagles and other birds patrol the emergent layer. They have sharp talons and powerful grips for plucking their prey out of the trees.

Fragility of the Rainforest Ecosystem

Despite their splendor, tropical rainforests are fragile. Everything is interdependent. Even minor changes to one part of the system can lead to widespread damage—or even complete destruction—of the whole.

Sadly, in the past century, humans have managed to destroy vast tracts of this precious resource. Rainforests once covered 14 percent of the earth's land surface. Now they cover less than 6 percent. Experts believe that the last remaining rainforests could be completely eradicated in less than 40 years. Over 200,000 acres of rainforest are burned every day.

What is the cause of this rapid destruction? Commercial logging is the single largest cause. Tropical hardwoods like teak, mahogany, and rosewood are used for furniture and building materials. The cardboard packing, wood chipboard, and paper industries are also large users of rainforest timber. The steel industry uses vast quantities of timber to make the charcoal needed to generate high heat for the smelting process.

Even more rainforest is destroyed by mining operations. Brazil, for example, sits on one of the world's largest reserves of iron ore. It also has gold, semiprecious and precious stones, natural gas, and oil reserves. The land is stripped to get at the ore. Water runs off the exposed land. It carries waste oil, mercury, and other contaminants throughout the region. Mercury, for example, runs off into the rivers and streams and is carried hundreds of miles. The result is the widespread poisoning of humans and animals.

Providing grazing land for animals is a third cause of deforestation. Most of Central and Latin America's rainforests, for example, has been lost to cattle operations to meet the world demand for meat.

Subsistence farming is yet another force behind the loss of rainforest land. As populations explode in Third World countries, the poor, hungry inhabitants seek new land to grow subsistence crops. They burn the rainforest in a process known as "slash-and-burn agriculture." Because the soil is generally poor, the land is exhausted by the time it has produced three or four crops. The homesteaders move on, slashing and burning more rainforest as they go. They leave behind fields of baked clay dotted with puddles of polluted water where once stood proud, towering forests of green.

Effects of Deforestation

Once an area of rainforest has been logged it can never become what it once was. Most of the time, the plants and animals of the original forest become extinct. Even if only sections of land are destroyed, these remnants change drastically. Birds and other animals cannot cross from one to another in the canopy, so plants are not pollinated, and seeds are not dispersed. Plants at the edges of the jungle lack the high humidity that they need to grow properly. As a result, the forest remnants gradually degrade and die. The thin topsoil, once protected by the canopy, washes away.

Massive deforestation brings with it many negative consequences. Air and water pollution, soil erosion, epidemics, and the decimation of indigenous Indian tribes are the most obvious results. No less important are the loss of biodiversity through extinction, and the release of carbon dioxide into the atmosphere. Fewer rainforests means less rain, less oxygen to breathe, and more global warming.

Choices we make can affect the progress of rainforest conservation or destruction. Using wood from sustainable sources, reducing consumption of forest products such as paper, and recycling aluminum cans (which come from the rainforest mineral, bauxite) are all ways students can make a practical difference in their everyday lives.

Information for the Student:
The Effects of Human Action on the Environment

Rainforests once covered 14 percent of Earth's surface. Today, they cover less than 6 percent. Experts estimate that if the current rate of destruction continues, by forty years from now, there will be virtually no natural rainforests left in the world.

In this unit, you will explore tropical rainforest ecosystems and what makes them unique. You will learn about how they are home to an incredible diversity of plant and animal species. You will also learn how they serve an important role in maintaining the balance of Earth's climate. You will also have the opportunity to explore how the rainforest is crucial in preventing "the greenhouse effect" and how your own actions can affect the future of the rainforest.

To succeed in this activity, you will need to do research using a variety of media and information sources. As you perform your research, keep in mind the following questions:

- Where are the best places to find the information I need? What types of materials will be the most useful?

- Is the source for my information reliable and accurate? Who is providing the information?

- Is the information relevant? How does this source help me answer the questions I am being asked or solve the problem I am being posed?

- How can I organize the information I find to make effective use of it when I need it?

- Did I record the sources of information I used so that I can create a bibliography?

- Did I collect all the information I need to prepare a presentation of my own?

Keep all of your work on this project—notes, worksheets, and reference information—together in a file folder or binder.

Student Worksheet 6-1

Name _____ Date _____

Tropical Rainforests of the World

Tropical rainforests can be found around the world. Use maps, atlases, and other reference materials to find out more about these rainforests. Choose at least **three** different types of sources, such as reference books, periodicals, Web sites, or encyclopedias.

Use the back of this sheet or your journal to take notes about the information that you find. Write down the name and bibliographic information for each source you use for future reference.

When you have completed your research, create a bibliography that lists all of your sources in alphabetical order. Then answer the following questions:

- List, in descending order, the largest tropical rainforests in the world. Note their location, size, and main characteristics. Also note how much land in each rainforest has disappeared since 1950.

  _____

- What must the annual rainfall be for a forest to be considered a rainforest?

  _____

- Near what latitude are most tropical rainforests found?

  _____

- What continents do NOT have tropical rainforests?

  _____

- What is a temperate rainforest, and how does it differ from a tropical rainforest?

  _____

Student Worksheet 6-2

Name _____ **Date** _____

Rainforest Residents

Choose one plant and one animal species that live in a tropical rainforest. Find out about your species' life cycles.

Choose at least **three** different types of sources, such as reference books, periodicals, Web sites, or encyclopedias.

Use the back of this sheet or your journal to take notes about the information that you find. Write down the name and bibliographic information for each source you use for future reference.

When you have completed your research, create a bibliography that lists all of your sources in alphabetical order. Then answer the following questions:

- What are the common and scientific names of your plant?

  _____

- Where does it live?

  _____

- Describe its life cycle.

  _____

- What are the common and scientific names of your animal?

  _____

- Where does it live?

  _____

- Describe its life cycle.

  _____

Student Worksheet 6-3

Name _____ **Date** _____

Layer Cake Diorama

Rainforests are composed of four main "layers." Research each of these layers. Determine what types of plants and animals live in each one.

For this activity, you will work as part of a group of four students. Choose the members of your group. Then choose a specific rainforest you wish to depict, for example, the Amazon. Build a four-layer diorama that illustrates this forest. Have each member of the group be responsible for one layer of the diorama.

Make sure all four layers connect in such a way as to illustrate the integrated nature of a rainforest. Make sure you include as much realistic, three-dimensional detail as possible in your diorama.

To ensure that your diorama is accurate, complete the following items before you begin construction.

- We are going to depict a rainforest in:

  _____

- The lowest layer of the rainforest is called _____.

  The following plants and animals live in this zone: _____

- The next layer of the rainforest is called _____.

  The following plants and animals live in this zone: _____

- The next layer of the rainforest is called _____.

  The following plants and animals live in this zone: _____

- The next layer of the rainforest is called _____.

  The following plants and animals live in this zone: _____

- Who will be responsible for each layer of the diorama? _____

- Who will be responsible for assembly of the diorama? _____

ASSESSMENT
Your diorama will be assessed based on the following criteria:
- **Accuracy:** the diorama is factually correct.
- **Creativity:** Your diorama is imaginatively and effectively produced.
- **Group cooperation:** Your diorama shows that all members of the group participated actively and equally.

Assessment for Diorama Group Project

Name _____ **Date** _____

Quality of Content

3   Tropical rainforest structure is clearly presented to the viewer. All levels are completely represented. Details are factually correct.

2   Tropical rainforest structure is unevenly presented to the viewer. Some levels are completely represented. Most details are factually correct.

1   Tropical rainforest structure is inadequately presented to the viewer. Levels are sketchily or incorrectly represented. Some details are factually correct.

Creativity

3   Diorama is creatively prepared and dramatically presented. Attention has been paid to overall concept and to details of construction. All levels are interrelated.

2   Diorama is of average creativity. Presentation lacks drama, but the overall concept is appealing. Details are not compelling. Levels are partially interrelated.

1   Diorama is workmanlike and betrays a lack of care. Little attention has been paid to the overall effect or to the details of the presentation. Layers are not related to one another.

Group Cooperation

3   All members of the group contributed at a high level to the completion of this project.

2   Some members of the group contributed at a high level. Others contributed marginally.

1   The group did not work together cooperatively to create this project. The result was a diorama that is largely the work of one or two people, or is a haphazard and poorly executed by an ineffective group.

Student Worksheet 6-4

Name _____ **Date** _____

Greenhouse Effect Lab

Because rainforests produce oxygen and absorb carbon dioxide, they are called "the lungs of the earth." They help regulate the temperature of Earth and maintain consistent climate zones around the world.

When rainforests are cut, they no longer absorb as much carbon dioxide from the atmosphere. Carbon dioxide builds up. The carbon dioxide traps heat. Gradually, the planet warms. This effect is known as the greenhouse effect.

In this experiment, you will duplicate the greenhouse effect. Perform the experiment. Record your results. Then answer the questions below.

Materials:

2 identical glass jars   1 clear plastic bag
1 liter cold water   thermometer
10 ice cubes

Procedure:

1. Pour 500 milliliters of cold water into each jar.
2. Add 5 ice cubes to each jar.
3. Place the plastic bag over jar 1 so that the jar opening is covered.
4. Leave both jars in the sun for one hour.
5. Measure the temperature of the water in each jar.

Jar 1 Temperature: _____ Jar 2 temperature: _____

Answer the following questions:

• After one hour, were the contents of one jar warmer than the other's contents? Why?

_____

• How does the plastic bag simulate carbon dioxide in the atmosphere?

_____

• How does this experiment relate to your study of the tropical rainforest?

_____

• How could planting more trees help counter the greenhouse effect?

_____

Part 2—Rainforest Rx

Background Information for the Teacher and Library Media Specialist

In part 2 of this unit, students will take a closer look at rainforest destruction and its causes. They will work independently to create a PowerPoint presentation that documents their findings about rainforest destruction. They will also present a plan for countering rainforest destruction.

Lesson Outline

Stimulate interest in this portion of the unit by asking students if they can explain why rainforests are shrinking around the world. Make a list on the blackboard of the suggestions offered by students. Explain that they will need to do research and collect data for a more accurate assessment of the causes.

Explain to students that there is a vast amount of information available on this subject. Ask students why that is so. Where is this information coming from? Have students use their critical faculties to determine why rainforest topics may be so popular at this time.

Ask students how they will collect data for this activity. What sources will they use? What obstacles might they encounter in trying to collect accurate data? Explain to students that not all sources of information will be objective. Ask students how they will evaluate information sources for bias and accuracy.

Advise students that the final step in this project will be to work independently to create a PowerPoint presentation that documents their findings about rainforest destruction. They will focus on one cause and demonstrate its effects on various rainforest systems around the world. Make sure students are familiar with the PowerPoint software before continuing with this unit.

Students will also be required to present a plan for countering rainforest destruction. For example, if they have been studying mining, they will offer a program to counter the effects of mining operations. Ask students how they will find this information. How will they evaluate whether a proposal is workable or fantastic? Is their plan something that individuals can do, or does it rely on government or other large agencies? How will they convince others to "buy in" to their plan?

Allow students to choose from the following categories for their presentations:

- Mining (gold, natural gas, bauxite)

- Grazing for cattle; meat production

- Timber for wood, paper, cardboard

- Subsistence agriculture

Information for the Student: Rainforest Rx

In part 1 of this activity, you researched rainforest ecosystems.

In part 2 of this activity, you will learn more about how the rainforests are being destroyed. You will also find out ways to prevent further destruction of this habitat.

To succeed in this activity, you will work independently to collect and record data. Then you will prepare a PowerPoint presentation that shows what you have learned about one cause of rainforest destruction. Your presentation will also include a proposal for overcoming this problem.

As you engage in your project, keep in mind the following questions:

- What information will I need for this project?

- Where are the best places to find the information I need? What types of materials will be the most useful? How can I evaluate the accuracy of my data sources?

- What organizational tools will best track the data and support my project?

- What materials will I need to create my PowerPoint presentation?

- How can I best present my findings in the PowerPoint format?

Student Worksheet 6-5

Name _____ **Date** _____

Protecting the Rainforest

Make a list of all the causes and suggestions you have found for offsetting rainforest destruction from the topic you are researching. Make sure you record the source for each suggestion.

Evaluate each suggestion. For each suggestion, ask yourself the following questions:

- Is it practical?

- Can this suggestion be implemented by individuals, or by governments and large businesses only?

- Will inhabitants of the region be in favor of this measure?

- Will the government of the region support this measure?

- Who would likely object to seeing this measure put in place? Is their argument against this measure valid? How could they be convinced to support this measure?

Choose the best suggestions for inclusion in your PowerPoint presentation.

Student Worksheet 6-6

Name _____ **Date** _____

Rainforest Activity: Self-Assessment

• During this project, I learned the following important information about the rainforest:

_____

• The most interesting thing I discovered about the rainforests of the world is:

_____

• As a result of this unit, I will be <u>more likely/less likely</u> to want to read the news about rainforests.

• As a result of this unit, I will be <u>more likely/less likely</u> to be careful about using rainforest resources.

• The work I did on my portion of the group diorama deserved this letter grade:

_____

Why? _____

_____

• The diorama my group produced deserved, as a whole, this letter grade: _____

Why? _____

• The most difficult part of this unit for me was: _____

• The part of this unit I liked the best was: _____

• My teachers were most helpful during this unit by: _____

• My teachers could have improved this unit by: _____

• My PowerPoint presentation deserved the following grade: _____

Why? _____

• During this unit, I learned that some sources of information can be unreliable because:

_____ (cite an example).

Assessment for PowerPoint Presentation

Name _____ **Date** _____

Quality of Content

3   Message is clear to the audience. All components support the presentation's main idea.

2   The audience is unsure of the main message of the presentation. Some components support the main idea. Others detract from the message.

1   No clear message is presented. Components bears little relation to the main idea.

Organization

3   Presentation is well organized. Audience follows the presentation. Order of presentation makes sense.

2   Presentation is somewhat organized. Audience seems somewhat confused.

1   Presentation is not well organized. Components do not have a coherent order. Graphics interferes with the message. Audience is very confused and loses interest.

Style

3   Presentation is given with flair. "Slides" are attractively prepared and dynamically presented.

2   Presentation is competent. "Slides" are adequate but not dynamic.

1   Presentation is sloppy. "Slides" are awkward and reveal a lack of preparation. Graphics are cursory and visually unexciting.

Mechanics

3   Entire presentation is smooth. Student understands how to use the technology and applies it properly.

2   Some parts of the presentation are smooth. Presenter is not entirely confident of how to use PowerPoint.

1   The presentation is not smoothly presented. Students seems uncomfortable with the PowerPoint software.

Organizational and Assessment Checklist for the Teacher

Lesson Component	Taught/Assessed by	Assessment Method
Introducing the Lesson —General Introduction • Identifying sources • How to prepare a bibliography		
Tropical Rainforests of the World		• Review Worksheet 6-1 answers for student comprehension of the material • Review bibliography for completeness and relevance of sources
Rainforest Residents		• Review Worksheet 6-2 answers for student comprehension of the material • Review bibliography for completeness and relevance of sources
Layer Cake Diorama		• Review Worksheet 6-3 answers for student comprehension of the material • Assess diorama
Greenhouse Effect Lab • Supervise lab activity		• Review Worksheet 6-4 answers for student comprehension of the material
Introduction to Part 2		
Protecting the Rainforest Rainforest Activity: Self-Assessment		• Review Worksheet 6-5 answers for student comprehension of the material • Review Worksheet 6-6 answers for student comprehension of the material
PowerPoint Presentation		Assessment for PowerPoint Presentation

Selected Suggested Resources/Bibliography

Items marked with an asterisk would be suitable for teacher background; all others would be for both teacher and student reference.

Web Sites

http://www.pineriver.k12.mi.us/ms/rainforest/rainforest.html
   Very useful guide prepared for/by a Michigan school district.

http://www.eduweb.com/amazon.html
   Info on where the Amazon is, how much rain a rainforest receives, who lives there, and how the native people earn a living.

http://jajhs.kana.k12.wv.us/amazon/
   Contains activities for students, raw data, links, journals, and virtual trips. Students may contribute to this site.

http://www.ran.org/ran/kids_action/index.html
   Explore the sights and sounds of the rainforest. Explores what kids are doing to protect these endangered habitats, and how students can make a difference.

http://www.msu.edu/~urquhar5/tour/index.html
   An interactive online tour of the rainforests of Central and South America, written for kids. It is an excellent source for part 2.

http://www.passporttoknowledge.com/rainforest/intro.html
   A virtual expedition into the planet's largest rainforest, guided by some of the world's leading biologists.

http://www.bagheera.com/inthewild/spot_sprain.htm
   Environmental site discusses why rainforests are important and what's destroying them.

http://www.bsrsi.msu.edu/rfrc/home.html
   Includes basics, geography, biology, deforestation, statistics, case studies, online rainforest tour, movies, and links.

http://www.oxfam.org.uk/coolplanet/ontheline/explore/nature/trfindex.htm
   Oxfam's site shows animals, plants, and people of the tropical rainforests. Explores why they're in danger, and what people are doing to protect them.

http://www.savetherainforest.org/
   Fact sheets, photos, and ideas about ways to help save the rainforest.

http://www.rainforestlive.org.uk
   An educational Web site on tropical rainforests. Links to projects, research, and expeditions. Chat rooms and teaching ideas.

http://www.blueplanetbiomes.org/rainforest.htm
   All about the tropical rainforest biome. Includes description, global position, climate, and information on specific plants and animals.

http://www.howstuffworks.com/rainforest.htm
   Photographic tour of a tropical rainforest shows what makes it such a rich environment for plants and animals.

http://greenkeepers.com/
>   56-page book about the rainforest can be downloaded and printed for offline reading. Site also includes Flash animated pages.

http://www.eliztaylor.freeserve.co.uk/Rainforest.html
>   Includes information on location, climate, animals, plants and products, indigenous inhabitants, deforestation, and environmental impact.

www.uwsp.edu/geo/faculty/ritter/geog101/
>   Very good overview of the geography of the rainforest.

modules/ecosystems_biomes/biomes_tropical_forests_page_2.html
>   *Variety in Abundance—Plants in the Rainforest.* This site discusses the different types of plants found in the rainforest and the rainforest ecosystem. Also information on the layers of the rainforest and the value of some of the plants found there.

www.rain-tree.com/
>   Hundreds of pages on the ecosystem of the rainforest, why it is valuable to us, why it is in danger, deforestation and logging, plants and medicines, the Amazon River, and indigenous peoples.

* http://www.efn.org/~dharmika/
>   Music and lesson plans on the rainforests.

http://mbgnet.mobot.org/sets/rforest/ind_Hlt80946058e_Hlt80946058x.htm
>   Simple exploration of rainforest geography, facts.

Print Resources

Baptista, L. H. *Discover Rainforests*. Lincolnwood, IL: Publications International, Ltd., 1992.

Gibbons, G. *Nature's Green Umbrella*. New York: William, 1992.

Goodman, B. *The Rain Forest*. New York: Tern Enterprise, Inc., 1991.

Greenaway, F. *Rain Forest*. New York: Dorling Kindersley, Inc., 1992.

Knapp, B. J. *What Do We Know About Rain Forests?* New York: Simon & Schuster Young Books (Peter Bedrick Books), 1992.

Landau, E. *Tropical Rain Forest: Around the World*. New York: Franklin Watts, 1990.

Sly, A. *The Brazilian Rain Forest*. New York: Dillon Press, 1992.

Visiting Pompeii and San Francisco: The Effects of Geologic Processes on Human Populations

Object of This Lesson

In this unit, students use library resources and a variety of research tools to explore the effects of geologic processes on people. They will learn, through studying the historic eruption of Mt. Vesuvius and the 1906 San Francisco earthquake, about cataclysmic processes of geology. Scientific experimentation will lead to a greater understanding of the mechanisms underlying these processes.

Students will then apply what they have learned to a study of earthquake preparedness. They will find out what measures are in place in various locations, such as Northern California, to protect populations from earthquakes.

This unit will support the following American Association for the Advancement of Science Benchmarks (p. 73):

- To understand that the interior of the earth is hot. Heat flow and movement of material with in the earth cause earthquakes and volcanic eruptions and create mountains and ocean basins. Gas and dust from large volcanoes can change the atmosphere.

- To recognize that some changes in the earth's surface are abrupt (such as earthquakes and volcano eruptions) while other changes happen very slowly (such as uplift and wearing down of mountains).

- To understand that earthquakes often occur along the boundaries between colliding plates.

Science Content Knowledge and Skills

Students will
- Describe orally and in writing how and why volcanoes erupt,
- Describe orally and in writing the causes of earthquakes,
- Locate Mt. Vesuvius and the San Andreas fault on a world map,
- Describe the effects of the two geologic events on human populations,
- Describe how buildings are affected by the shaking of the ground that happens during earthquakes,
- Create a model of a volcano or a fault line, and
- Create a "shake table" and test various structures for earthquake resistance.

Information Literacy Knowledge and Skills

Students will

- Use a variety of different index types to locate material;
- Describe how they found and chose their resources;
- Evaluate the appropriateness of the research material;
- Identify three different types of media used to find the information required;
- Prepare a complete bibliography;
- Describe the difference between a primary and a secondary source;
- Explain how fact, point of view, and opinions are different from one another;
- Present information in a clear and organized manner; and
- Present information creatively.

Lesson Outline

This lesson is designed to be team-taught by a library media specialist and a science specialist. Before you introduce the lesson to students, decide which aspects of the unit will be presented by each member of the team. Decide who will assess student performance on each component of the unit. Use the checklist at the end of this chapter to assist you in organizing these aspects of teaching this unit.

Stimulate interest in the lesson by asking students if they have ever experienced an earthquake or a volcano eruption. Share stories and recollections.

Explain to students that you will be leading a research project into how earthquakes and volcano eruptions affect people. Explain that you will begin your study with an examination of two very famous events—the eruption of Mt. Vesuvius in 79 A.D. and the San Francisco Earthquake of 1906.

Explain that the students will be conducting research into the subject by consulting many different types of sources. Ask students where they might find information on this topic. Create a list of possible sources of information on the blackboard.

Describe the differences between types of sources. Can students identify a primary source versus a secondary source? Define each term. Which term would refer to an eyewitness account? Direct students to keep a record of the definition in their journals.

Point out the list of sources on the blackboard. Ask students how they would find the appropriate materials in each category. Make sure students understand how to use the various indexing tools available in your information center.

Ask students what sources they would trust the most when reviewing information. Which sources would they trust the least? Offer suggestions: a museum or historical society Web site, a high school student's term paper posted on the Web, a local newspaper report, a scientific journal.

Ask students how they will organize the information they collect. Brainstorm methods and materials to help in the organization and retrieval of data for this project.

Reinforce the concept of the bibliography. How will a bibliography help students keep track of their data? How else will a bibliography be useful?

Go over the proper format of bibliographical entries for different types of resources. Make sure students know which information is important for the bibliography and which information is not required. Also show students where the necessary information can be located, for example, in the front of a book or at the bottom of a Web page.

Ask students if they have any questions about how to proceed with the first step of the project. Review as needed. It may be helpful to list all the steps required for completion of this project on the blackboard. Encourage students to use Research Project Checklist 1 (Student Worksheet 1-A) as a model for keeping track of their work.

Part 1—Visiting Pompeii and San Francisco

Background Information for the Teacher and Library Media Specialist

Mt. Vesuvius is an active volcano in Italy. It lies above a subduction zone—a zone where one geologic plate is moving under another. As it moves to the north at a rate of two to three centimeters per year, the African plate is being pushed beneath the Eurasian plate, causing instability in the region.

Vesuvius has erupted many times in its history, causing enormous damage to the surrounding area. The most famous eruption, however, was the one that occurred on the morning of August 24, 79.

The citizens of Pompeii, the city at the base of the mountain, were not alarmed by the first sighting of a column of smoke rising from the mountain. There had been several other eruptions that had caused damage to the city. But the damage had been repaired, and life went on. No one expected this eruption to be any different.

But this eruption *was* different. It had two distinct phases. First there was a the *Plinian* phase, during which material was ejected in a tall column, then spread through the atmosphere and fell to earth like rain. Next came a *Peléan* phase, in which material flowed down the sides of the volcano in fast-moving avalanches of gas and dust called *pyroclastic flow*.

The Plinian eruption of Vesuvius began at midday. It created a column of smoke approximately 20 kilometers (66,000 feet) high. A rain of ash and pumice covered a broad area to the south of the mountain. This phase lasted about 18 hours and deposited about 2.5 meters (8.2 feet) of pumice stones on Pompeii. While the pumice and rock were too small to injure people, the combined weight of the fallout was enough to cause roofs to collapse.

Most of the 20,000 residents of Pompeii had fled the city by the next morning. Only 2,000 or so remained in the town for the next, and more deadly, phase of the eruption.

The Peléan phase brought an avalanche of pumice, ash, and gasses, the pyroclastic flow, tumbling down the mountain. The super hot cloud of steam and mud completely covered the town of Herculaneum. It took only about four minutes for the boiling mud to flow from Vesuvius to Herculaneum, a distance of about seven kilometers (four miles). Subsequent waves reached Pompeii, asphyxiating those who had survived the fall of 3 meters (10 feet) of pumice and were fleeing across the open in the dark or hiding beneath roofs. The waves that followed smashed flat the upper floors of houses and left the corpses encased in successive blankets of lava and ash.

The cities of Pompeii and Herculaneum were completely destroyed, the ruins entombed by a thick layer of ash. They remained undisturbed for hundreds of years until archeologists began to piece together the lives of the one-time residents.

San Francisco, 1906

Nearly 2,000 years separate the eruption of Mt. Vesuvius from the San Francisco earthquake of 1906. But both events share similarities: a lack of concern over preliminary tremors, a sense of panic as the destruction mounted, and a widespread loss of life and property.

At 5:12 A.M. on April 18, the first foreshock occurred. It was felt widely throughout the San Francisco Bay area. The earthquake itself broke loose some 20 to 25 seconds later. It was felt from southern Oregon to south of Los Angeles, and inland as far as central Nevada. The shaking lasted for about a minute and was punctuated by violent shocks.

Almost immediately after the shock, fires broke out in San Francisco. The fire lasted three days and caused substantially more damage than did the earthquake. The burned area covered 4.7 square miles and included residential, factory, and commercial districts.

It is estimated that the earthquake caused 3,000 deaths, directly or indirectly; 28,000 buildings were destroyed, 225,000 people were left homeless, and more than $400,000,000 worth of property was damaged.

What caused such a large quake? Like Pompeii, the San Francisco Bay area lies along a boundary between two large geologic plates. The Pacific Plate (on the west) moves northwestward relative to the North American Plate (on the east). The boundary line is called the San Andreas fault. The entire San Andreas fault system is more than 800 miles long. It extends to depths of at least 10 miles within the earth.

During the 1906 earthquake, the San Andreas fault "slipped." Roads, fences, and rows of trees and bushes that crossed the fault were offset several yards. The road across the head of Tomales Bay was offset almost 21 feet, the maximum offset ever recorded.

Modern Developments

The 1906 earthquake provided a wealth of information about earthquakes. Researchers, using data from the quake, were able to piece together the first theory of why and how earthquakes happen. Using that data, they have been able to craft a plan for earthquake preparedness in geologically active regions such as San Francisco and Vesuvius. Instruments and repeated surveys track the plate motion and the related stressing and distortion of the earth's crust (which causes earthquakes). Data are analyzed with the aid of computers. From this understanding, maps have been created that predict where shaking is likely to be strong. The maps are used to make land use decisions, such as where to locate schools, hospitals, homes, and nuclear power plants. Engineers use the data to develop building codes for buildings and bridges that can withstand the shaking.

Today, cities that lie in geologically active areas are still at risk from cataclysmic events like volcano eruptions and earthquakes. However, a better understanding of the processes behind them may help residents of these areas escape the fate of Pompeiians or San Franciscans of the past.

Information for the Student: The Effects of Geologic Processes on Human Populations

Imagine you are a citizen of Pompeii in the year 79 A.D. A plume of smoke is rising from the nearby volcano, Mt. Vesuvius.

Do you pack your bags and run? Or calmly wait for the danger to pass? In this unit, you will explore what actually happened in Pompeii in that fateful year. You will also learn about another geological event, the San Francisco earthquake of 1906. You will find out what these two events had in common, and how they differed.

To succeed in this activity, you will need to do research using a variety of media and information sources. As you perform your research, keep in mind the following questions:

- Where are the best places to find the information I need? What types of materials will be the most useful?

- Is the source for my information reliable and accurate? Who is providing the information?

- Is the information relevant? How does this source help me answer the questions I am being asked or solve the problem I am being posed?

- How can I organize the information I find to make effective use of it when I need it?

At the end of this unit, you will need to prepare a bibliography of the sources you used to find the information you need. A bibliography is a summary of the documents you used. The materials are described using a standard format so that other people can find the same information you did and conduct their own research into the topic.

As you work, make sure you record the following information about your sources. You should record:

- The title of the book, article, video, or web page you used;

- The complete name of the author;

- The publisher of the book or article, the producer of the video, or the Web site address;

- The date of publication or the date the material was produced; and

- The city in which the material was produced or published.

Collecting this information as you do your research will save you a great deal of time later. It will also help you locate information again if you need to refer back to something.

Keep all of your work on this project —notes, worksheets, and reference information— together in a file folder or binder.

Student Worksheet 7-1

Name _____ **Date** _____

Pompeii, A.D. 79

Mt. Vesuvius erupted in A.D. 79, completely destroying the cities of Pompeii and Herculaneum.

Use at least **six** different sources to find out more about this event. Choose at least **three** different types of sources, such as reference books, periodicals, Web sites, or encyclopedias. Use at least **one** primary source.

Use the back of this sheet to make a list of questions to help guide your work. Check them off as you find the answers to each one. Write down the name and bibliographic information for each source for future reference.

When you have completed your research, create a bibliography that lists all of your sources in alphabetical order. Highlight your primary sources. Then answer the following questions:

- Where is Mt. Vesuvius? Draw a map or diagram, complete with labels.

  _____

- Who was Pliny? Why is he important to our knowledge of Pompeii and volcano eruptions?

  _____

- Describe, in your own words, the two stages of Mt. Vesuvius's eruption.

  _____

- Describe, in your own words, why you think some people remained in Herculaneum and Pompeii after the first plume of smoke was spotted.

  _____

- Explain why Mt. Vesuvius is geologically active.

  _____

- Do you think Mt. Vesuvius will erupt again? Why or why not? Explain your answer.

  _____

Student Worksheet 7-2

Name _____ **Date** _____

San Francisco, 1906

A massive earthquake struck the San Francisco Bay area on the morning of April 18, 1906.

Use at least **six** different sources to find out more about this event. Choose at least **three** different types of sources, such as reference books, periodicals, Web sites, or encyclopedias. Use at least **three** primary sources.

Use the back of this sheet to make a T-chart to help organize your work. List the types of resources you will need. Check them off as you find and read them. Write down the name of each source and other details for future reference.

When you have completed your research, create a bibliography that lists all of your sources in alphabetical order. Highlight your primary sources. Then answer the following questions:

- What and where is the San Andreas fault? Draw a map or diagram, complete with labels. Highlight San Francisco and Santa Rosa on your map.

  _____

- Describe, in your own words, what happened in San Francisco during the period from April 18–21, 1906.

  _____

- Why did a fire break out in San Francisco?

  _____

- Explain why the San Andreas fault is geologically active.

  _____

- Do you think there will be another earthquake in San Francisco as damaging as the one in 1906? Why or why not? Explain your answer.

  _____

Student Worksheet 7-3

Name _____ **Date** _____

Comparing Pompeii and San Francisco

Use what you have learned about the geologic events in Pompeii in 79 A.D. and San Francisco in 1906 to answer the following questions:

• How do you think these two events were similar? _____

_____

How were they different? _____

_____

• Which do you think is more deadly: an earthquake or a volcano eruption? Why?

_____

• Knowing what you know now, what would you have done if you had been in Pompeii that morning? In San Francisco?

_____

• Do you think you would like to live near Mt. Vesuvius today? _____

_____

San Francisco? _____

Explain your answers. _____

_____

Student Worksheet 7-4

Name _____ **Date** _____

Creating a Timeline

Choose either San Francisco or Mt. Vesuvius. Draw a timeline that shows the major geologic events that have happened in this location.

Include other world events, such as "Columbus discovers America," on your timeline.

Part 2—The Effects of Geologic Processes on Human Populations

Background Information for the Teacher and Library Media Specialist

In part 2 of this unit, students will apply what they have learned about earthquakes and volcano eruptions to explore earthquake preparedness and safety.

Lesson Outline

Stimulate interest in this portion of the unit by asking students how some of the damage caused by the volcano eruptions and earthquakes of the past could have been prevented. Point out that roofs collapsed in Pompeii from the weight of pumice and ash. Buildings in San Francisco collapsed because they were severely shaken, thanks in part to loose soil. Power and gas lines were severed by the quake, causing fires that were even more damaging than the quake itself.

Explain to students that they will be investigating how to prevent severe damage in the future. Explain that they will do lab activities to test various structures for earthquake resistance. They will then prepare reports on safety measures in place in modern cities such as San Francisco. Allow students to choose their partners for this project.

Tell students that lab work requires accuracy in measurement and in reporting. Detailed note-taking is an important part of the process. Have the science teacher show students how to prepare a laboratory report that details their procedures, materials, and results. Explain to students that someone who reads their lab report should be able to duplicate their experiment and get the same results.

Ask students if they have any questions about how to proceed with the lab activities. Review as needed. It may be helpful to list all the steps required for completion of each activity on the blackboard. Encourage students to create their own checklist of steps to keep track of their work.

Information for the Student: Tips for Building Structures

- Try cross or diagonal bracing to stabilize your building. Cross-bracing means you put in vertical "X' shaped braces between the popsicle stick walls.

- Try different materials for your cross braces and see which works best. Possibilities for cross bracing include popsicle sticks, kite string, and straws.

- To simulate masonry structures made of brick, stone, or adobe, use sugar cubes for the bricks and peanut butter, frosting, or double-sided tape for the mortar. Use a piece of Styrofoam or cardboard scraps for the buildings' bases, second stories, and roofs.

- To strengthen buildings, carefully attach scraps of window screening to the inside walls of the first stories using a thin layer of extra "mortar." Reinforce by putting extra "mortar" at the inside corners and joins.

- Try building structures in different geometric shapes. Consider L-shapes, P-shapes, or T-shapes.

- Test and compare buildings of one story and of two stories.

- Model steel frame, high-rise structures using pipe cleaners, T-pins, and Styrofoam. Bend the end of one pipe cleaner around the end of the other. Do not twist the ends together. Attach each model to a Styrofoam base with T-pins. Make cardboard or paper walls and add them to your structure.

Information for the Student: The Effects of Geologic Processes on Human-Made Structures

In part 1 of this unit, you researched two of the major events in geologic history.

In part 2 of this unit, you will apply what you have learned to lab experiments that will evaluate the effects of earthquakes and volcano eruptions on human-made structures.

To succeed in this activity, you will work with a partner to research the topic. You will do lab work to test some model structures. You will do a written report that describes modern methods of earthquake preparedness and safety. As you do your lab work and prepare for your report, keep in mind the following questions:

- What information will I need to do my report?

- Where are the best places to find the information I need? What types of materials will be the most useful?

- What visual materials will best show the data and support my report? (Consider charts, illustrations, photographs, and diagrams.)

- How can I organize the information I find to make a clear and exciting presentation?

Student Worksheet 7-5

Name _____ Date _____

Building a Shake Table

Materials:
    marbles
    plastic lid from a coffee can
    shoebox
    staples and stapler
    scissors

Procedure:

1. Cut the base out of the bottom of the shoebox. Trim each side by approximately 1/4 inch so that the cardboard will be able to fit inside the lid of the shoebox and slide about slightly.

2. Staple the plastic coffee can lid, lip up, to the cardboard cut from the shoebox bottom.

3. Place the cardboard with the coffee can lid, lid side down, into the shoebox cover.

4. Put marbles under the coffee can lid. The cardboard sheet should roll on the marbles inside the box top.

This is your "shaker table." You will use this to test various structures for resistance to shaking such as occurs during an earthquake.

Student Worksheet 7-6

Name _____ Date _____

Shaker Test Worksheet 1

Build a variety of structures using toothpicks, pasta shapes, marshmallows, wire, sugar cubes, peanut butter "mortar," etc.

Test each structure by affixing it to your shaker table (use peanut butter or honey to hold it in place.) Then, shake the shoebox lid in various directions (side to side, up and down), at various intensities, and for varying durations.

Record the results of each trial on a data record sheet. Make sure to record the time of the experiment, the materials used, the exact procedure used for each trial, and the outcome for each trial.

Student Names _____ Date _____

Experiment Name: _____

Materials Used: _____

Trial #	Trial Procedure	Outcome
1	Shook up and down	Collapsed
2	Shook side to side	Fell over sideways
3		

Then answer the following questions:

- What was the most damaging form of shaking (e.g., long waves, short, sharp waves, vertical waves, side-to-side waves)?

  _____

- Which structure was the most stable under all conditions? The least stable?

  _____

- What would you do to improve the results of your experiments if you were to repeat them?

  _____

- Which do you think is more important to building stability—the materials used or the shape of the structure? Why?

  _____

142

Student Worksheet 7-7

Name _____ Date _____

Shaker Test Worksheet 2: Roof Strength

Build a variety of structures using toothpicks, pasta shapes, marshmallows, wire, sugar cubes, peanut butter "mortar," etc. Make sure to include a variety of roof shapes and materials.

Test each structure by placing it inside a deep-sided container (to contain mess). Gradually pour up to four cups (one liter) of sand onto each structure.

How much weight can your rooftops sustain before collapsing? Record the results of each trial on a data record sheet. Make sure to record the time of the experiment, the materials used, the exact procedure used for each trial, and the outcome for each trial.

Then, answer the following questions:

- Which was the strongest roof? The weakest?

  _____

  _____

  _____

- What would you do to improve the results of your experiments if you were to repeat them?

  _____

  _____

  _____

- Which do you think is more important to roof failure—the materials used or the shape of the roof? Why?

  _____

  _____

  _____

Student Worksheet 7-8

Name _____ **Date** _____

Earthquake Preparedness Report

Research the ways in which one municipality such as San Francisco has dealt with the threat of earthquakes or other geological events. Write a report that describes the city's measures. Then offer an opinion about whether the measures described will be effective during an earthquake or volcano eruption of great magnitude.

Your report should include:

- A title that describes your main ideas;

- A standard report format, with an introduction, body paragraphs, and conclusion;

- Detailed sources for each piece of information you cite;

- References to your study of Pompeii and San Francisco, and your lab experiments; and

- Graphs, maps, or diagrams as appropriate.

Your report should answer the following questions:

- What agencies are responsible for earthquake preparedness in this location?

- What measures have they taken?

- Are the measures adequate? Why or why not?

- What more could the city or town do to protect its citizens during an earthquake or volcanic eruption?

- Would you want to live in this city or town? Why or why not?

Assessment for Written Presentation

Name _____ Date _____

Quality of Content

3   Information is comprehensive and clearly presented. Diagrams support the report's main idea.

2   Information presented is of moderate depth and interest. Presentation is adequate. Some graphics support the main idea. Others detract from the message.

1   Content is weak and poorly presented. Diagrams are not included or bear little relation to the main idea.

Organization

3   Report is well organized. Order of presentation makes sense. Introduction, body paragraphs, and conclusion are present.

2   Presentation is somewhat organized. Paragraphs are present but are not consistent in content or structure.

1   Presentation is not well organized. Formal structure is absent.

Style

3   Report is written with flair. Transitions between paragraphs and between types of material are effective. Graphics are attractively prepared and dynamically presented.

2   Report is competent. Transitions between topics are occasionally rocky. Graphics are adequate but not dynamic.

1   Report is sloppy. Transitions between paragraphs are nonexistent. Graphics are cursory or not present.

Organizational and Assessment Checklist for the Teacher

Lesson Component	Taught/Assessed by	Assessment Method
Introducing the Lesson —General Introduction • Identifying sources • How to prepare a bibliography		
Pompeii, A.D. 79		• Review Worksheet 7-1 answers for student comprehension of the material • Review bibliography for completeness and relevance of sources
San Francisco, 1906		• Review Worksheet 7-2 answers for student comprehension of the material • Review bibliography for completeness and relevance of sources
Comparing Pompeii and San Francisco		• Review Worksheet 7-3 answers for student comprehension of the material
Creating a Timeline		• Review timeline for student comprehension of the material and accuracy
Introduction to Part 2		
Building a Shake Table		
Shaker Test Worksheet 1		• Review data collection sheet • Review Worksheet 7-6 answers for student comprehension of material
Shaker Test Worksheet 2		• Review data collection sheet • Review Worksheet 7-7 answers for student comprehension of material
Earthquake Preparedness Report		Assessment for Written Presentation

Selected Suggested Resources/Bibliography

Items marked with an asterisk would be suitable for teacher background; all others would be for both teacher and student reference.

Web Sites

http://www.exploratorium.edu/faultline/ls/index.html
> Top quality information from the Exploratorium's Living on the Faultline Project on earthquake causes, plus lab activities for investigating many aspects of earthquakes. Shake table models and activities.

http://pubs.usgs.gov/gip/earthq3/what.html
> Government documents prepared for educational purposes describe the San Andreas fault.

http://volcano.und.nodak.edu/vwdocs/volc_images/img_vesuvius.html
> Photos and drawings of Mt. Vesuvius and surrounding area.

http://mceer.buffalo.edu/education/exercises/struct.asp
> Multidisciplinary Center for Earthquake Engineering Research has complete instructions for building structures to test on shake tables.

http://www.eeri.org/cds_publications/earthquake_basics_series.html
> Free downloadable briefs (in Acrobat) covering liquefaction and insuring against natural disasters.

http://www.bbc.co.uk/history/ancient/romans/pompeii_rediscovery_01.shtml
> Pompeii: Its Discovery and Preservation.

http://www.bbc.co.uk/history/ancient/romans/pompeii_art_gallery.shtml
> Pompeii art and architecture.

http://www.bbc.co.uk/history/ancient/romans/daily_life_gallery.shtml
> Work and Play in Everyday Pompeii.

http://www.bbc.co.uk/history/historic_figures/pliny_the_younger.shtml
> Bio of Pliny the Younger.

http://www.bbc.co.uk/history/ancient/romans/rome_timeline.shtml
> Ancient Rome timeline.

http://www.bbc.co.uk/radio4/history/inourtime/inourtime_20030703.shtml
> BBC Radio 4 summary of program on vulcanology.

http://www.thecolefamily.com/italy/pompeii/
> Pompeii virtual tour.

http://www.pompeiisites.org/database/pompei/pompei2.nsf
> Official site of the Soprintendenza di Pompei.

http://volcanoes.usgs.gov/Products/Pglossary/fumarole.html
> Photo glossary of volcano terms.

http://www.imss.fi.it/pompei/index.html
> Pompeii virtual exhibition.

http://quake.wr.usgs.gov/info/basics.html
    Superb basic information on earthquakes.

http://earthquake.usgs.gov/4kids/
    Basic earthquake information for a younger audience.

Print Resources

Berry, J., ed. *Unpeeling Pompeii*. Milan, Italy: Electa, 1998.

Black, B. "Quake-proof Building." *Scholastic News* (March 9, 1990): Explorer Edition 4, Hands-on Science Supplement.

"Bracing for the Big One." *Superscience Blue* (October 1990) 15–17.

Chayet, B. "Bending without Breaking." *Scholastic News* (March 9, 1990): Citizen Edition 5, Hands-on Science Supplement.

Hilston, P., and C. R. Hilston. *A Field Guide to Planet Earth: Projects for Reading Rocks, Rivers, Mountains, and the Forces That Shape Them*. Chicago: Chicago Review Press, 1993.

Levy, M., and M. Salvadori. *Why Buildings Fall Down: Structures Fail*. New York: W. W. Norton, 1992.

Nappo, S. C. *Pompeii: Guide to the Lost City*. London: Weidenfeld & Nicolson, 1998.

Salvadori, M. *The Art of Construction: Projects and Principles for Beginning Engineers and Architects*. Chicago: Chicago Review Press, 1990.

Wallace-Hadrill, A. *Houses and Society in Pompeii and Herculaneum*. Princeton, NJ: Princeton University Press, 1994.

All ri...
Printed in ...

Looking at Light:
An Investigation of the Composition
of Sunlight and Human Vision

Object of This Lesson

In this unit, students use library resources and a variety of research tools to explore the subjects of light and how human vision operates. They will learn, through scientific experimentation, about the composition of sunlight, colors, reflection, refraction, and the structure of the eye.

Concurrently, students will engage in a survey of various media (print and television) to find out how light and optics are used in the world of technology. They will also explore how the media portray different subjects and for different purposes using visual and other techniques.

This unit will support the following American Association for the Advancement of Science Benchmarks (p. 90, p. 91, p. 137):

- To understand that light from the sun is made up of a mixture of many different colors of light, even though, to the eye, the light looks almost white.

- To understand that other things that give off or reflect light have a different mix of colors.

- To recognize that something can be "seen" when light waves emitted or reflected by it enter the eye.

- To recognize the effect of wavelength on how waves interact with matter, for example, what causes the sky to look blue or sunsets to appear red.

- To recognize that interaction between the eyes, nerves and brain are responsible for vision, and that this interaction helps make learning possible.

Science Content Knowledge and Skills

Students will

- Describe orally, graphically, and in writing the structure of the human eye;

149

- Describe and demonstrate the composition of sunlight;

- Describe and demonstrate the purpose and function of a prism;

- Create models that describe and demonstrate the effects of sunlight in forming rainbows, blue skies, and red sunsets;

- Measure temperature accurately; and

- Record scientific data appropriately.

Information Literacy Knowledge and Skills

Students will

- Assess whether a range of information problems or questions can be resolved based on one's own knowledge or whether additional information is required;

- Recognize that accurate and comprehensive information is the basis for intelligent decision making;

- State both broad and specific questions that will help in finding needed information;

- Use a full range of information sources to locate material;

- Explain and apply a plan to access needed information;

- Judge the accuracy, relevance, and completeness of sources and information in relation to a range of topics and information problems;

- Judge and support judgments of the degree of inaccuracy, bias, or misleading information in information sources and products;

- Integrate accurate, relevant, and comprehensive information to resolve an information problem or question;

- Organize information for practical application;

- Integrate new information into their own knowledge;

- Produce and communicate information and ideas in appropriate formats;

- Seek information from diverse sources and contexts;

- Present information in a clear and organized manner; and

- Devise strategies for revising, improving and updating self-generated knowledge.

Lesson Outline

This lesson is designed to be team-taught by a library media specialist and a science specialist. Before you introduce the lesson to students, decide which aspects of the unit will be presented by each member of the team. Decide who will assess student performance on each component of the unit. Use the checklist at the end of this chapter to assist you in organizing these aspects of teaching the unit.

Stimulate interest in the lesson by asking students what they know about light, color, and optics. Make a list on the blackboard (in one column, if possible, on the left side of the blackboard) of the responses.

Explain to students that you will be leading a research project into these topics. To help organize and guide their work on this project, students will be using a tool called a K-W-L chart.

Draw a sample of the K-W-L chart pictured on Student Worksheet 8-1 on the blackboard. Place the "K" column header above the list of the student responses to your initial question. Explain that the K stands for what you already **k**now about this subject.

Make a second column header and label it W. Say that that W stands for What, for example, what else one would like to know about this subject. Ask for student contributions to this column. If there are none, add your own, such as the following questions:

- Why is the sky blue?

- Why are sunsets red?

- Why do spoons appear bent when they are stuck in a glass of water?

- How do our eyes work to gather information from light?

- Do all animals see the way we do?

- What is a wavelength?

Solicit any further contributions to column W at this point.

Next, create a third column with a header labeled L. Explain to students that the L stands for Learned, that is, what they have *learned* as a result of this activity. Tell students that they will be filling in this column as they progress through the research project.

Pass out copies of the reproducible K-W-L chart. Have students label the worksheets with their names and the date. Have students add a title to describe the first research experiment they will do. For example, if you intend to begin this unit with the experiment on Student Worksheet 8-2, have students label the worksheet "Parts of the Eye." Tell students there will be additional K-W-L charts provided as needed throughout this unit.

Have students begin to fill out their charts. They may use any appropriate information from the blackboard for columns K and W.

Stress that, at this point, it does not matter whether the information in the K column is correct or accurate. Students will have the opportunity to revise any information in the K column as they learn more about the subject.

Have students list strategies for answering the questions in column W or finding information on this topic on the back of this sheet or in their science journals. Remind students that some information can come from books or other reference materials, some can come from other people, such as classmates, and some can come from direct observation or experimentation.

Explain as well that when doing science, each new piece of information usually stimulates further questions. As information is added to the L column, more questions for the W column will arise. Add these questions to that column as you work. Students may find that one or more of these questions stimulates interest in a topic that will serve for the research project described on Student Worksheet 8-7.

Ask students how they will organize the information they collect. Brainstorm methods and materials to help in the organization and retrieval of data for this project. Introduce the concept of the bibliography. How will a bibliography help students keep track of their data? How else will a bibliography be useful?

Go over the proper format of bibliographical entries for different types of resources. Make sure students know which information is important for the bibliography and which information is not required. Also show students where the necessary information can be located, for example, in the front of a book or at the bottom of a Web page.

Ask students if they have any questions about how to use their K-W-L charts while doing the experiments in part 1. Review as needed. It may be helpful to create a checklist of all the steps required for completion of this project on the blackboard. Encourage students to use the checklist of steps to keep track of their work in their journal.

Student Worksheet 8-1

Name _____ Date _____

K-W-L Chart for Topic:

K	W	L
_____	_____	_____
_____	_____	_____
_____	_____	_____
_____	_____	_____
_____	_____	_____
_____	_____	_____
_____	_____	_____
_____	_____	_____
_____	_____	_____
_____	_____	_____
_____	_____	_____
_____	_____	_____
_____	_____	_____
_____	_____	_____
_____	_____	_____
_____	_____	_____
_____	_____	_____
_____	_____	_____
_____	_____	_____
_____	_____	_____
_____	_____	_____

Part 1—Experimenting with Light and Vision

Background Information for the Teacher and Library Media Specialist

Electromagnetic radiation is the main way that energy is carried through the universe. Heat, radio waves, x-rays, and ultraviolet rays are all examples of electromagnetic radiation. Light is the *visible* part of the electromagnetic spectrum.

In the 17th century, the Dutch physicist Christiaan Huygens was the first to propose that light traveled, like sound, in the form of waves. This view of light formed the basis for most of our understanding until the 20th century. It was only then that scientists working in the fields of nuclear science discovered that light possesses a curious duality. At times, it behaves like a wave. At others, it behaves like a particle. After a great deal of experimentation, light particles, or *photons,* were identified by Albert Einstein in 1905.

Properties of Light

The Wavelength

The behaviors and properties of electromagnetic radiation are affected by wavelength. Radiation with relatively long waves (and low energy) is best recognized in the form of radio. Visible light is much shorter and has more energy. The shortest form of electromagnetic radiation is gamma waves. Gamma waves arise from the decay of nuclear components at the center of the atom. Gamma particles contain the greatest amount of energy of any photon.

Reflection

An incoming light wave is referred to as an *incident* wave. Reflections occur when incident waves meet a boundary that does not absorb their energy. The surface bounces the waves away. The bounced wave is called the *reflected* wave. The simplest example of visible light reflection is the glassy surface of a smooth body of water that reflects the scenery around it.

Refraction

Light can be bounced, or reflected. It can also be bent, or *refracted*. Light generally travels in a straight line. However, when it meets a boundary at more or less than a 90 degree angle, the beam of light will bend. How much it bends will depend on the degree of the angle and the material through which the beam of light is passing.

Light can also be split, or dispersed, into its component wavelengths. Lenses and prisms are tools designed for this purpose.

Light and the Human Eye

Human stereo color vision is a very complex process. Despite hundreds of years of study and experimentation, it is still not completely understood. What makes it so complex is that vision involves the nearly simultaneous interaction of two eyes and the brain, plus a network of neurons, receptors, and other specialized cells.

The basic process is as follows: Light enters the eye, passing through the cornea, pupil, and lens. The iris controls the amount of light that enters the eye. The iris is the colored "ring" you can see when you look into someone's eyes.

Light, focused by the lens, falls on the retina at the back of the eyeball. There, the light stimulates photoreceptors. These receptors can be either rod- or cone-shaped. Rods are most responsive in low light conditions. Cones are most responsive to color and in bright conditions.

The rods and cones convert the stimuli into electrical signals. The optic nerves transmit the electrical signals from each eye to the brain. The brain then processes the signals in several stages. The final destination of the signals is the visual cortex. It is located in the cerebrum.

It is only after the information has been processed in the visual cortex that we can comprehend what we see. If your eyes function perfectly, but your visual cortex is damaged, you cannot see.

What We See When We See

Light visible to humans is usually composed of a mixture of wavelengths. The composition of these wavelengths can vary depending on the source of the light. Of course the greatest source of light on Earth is the sun. The human eye has adapted uniquely to this light source.

Our eyes are sensitive to only a narrow band of electromagnetic radiation. The band lies in the wavelength range between 400 and 700 nanometers. This band is commonly called the *visible light spectrum.* When combined, all of the wavelengths in this spectrum meld to produce a colorless white light.

Color is the most noticeable aspect of light. Colors are usually caused by the way objects reflect or absorb light. The reason something like a leaf appears green, for instance, is because the leaf absorbs all colors except green. The green wavelengths are reflected back to our eyes. We see a green leaf.

Similarly, the sky appears blue because all other colors bounce off the atmosphere and back into space. Only the blue passes through the atmosphere and into our eyes.

The colors that make up white light are red, orange, yellow, green, blue, indigo, and violet. (A common mnemonic device to remember the colors and their order is to arrange the first letters of each into the name "ROY. G. BIV.") Red is the longest wave. Violet is the shortest.

The colors red, green, and blue are fundamental to human vision. They are called primary colors. All other colors are combinations of these three basic shades.

Although we cannot *see* all wavelengths, we can *feel* some of them. Heat is also known as infrared radiation. Infrared radiation has a longer wavelength than visible light.

Animals can see different portions of the electromagnetic spectrum. Honeybees, for example, can detect ultraviolet light.

Binocular Vision

Another feature of human vision is our ability to see in stereo. Our eyes, placed close together on the front of our faces, see slightly different images. These two images combine in the brain to give us a three-dimensional view of the world.

Parts of the Eye

Aqueous humor	The clear, watery fluid found in the front chamber of the eye.
Choroid	Layer of blood vessels that nourish the eye. Also absorbs light.
Cones	Photoreceptors in the retina that are most active in bright light conditions. Responsible for color vision.
Cornea	Transparent tissue that covers the front of the eye.

Iris	Circular band of muscles that controls the size of the pupil.
Lens	Transparent, flexible tissue that focuses light onto the retina by bending it as it passing through the eye.
Optic nerve	Conduit from the retina to the brain that carries the electrical signals produced by light falling on the rods and cones.
Pupil	Opening in the center of the eye through which light passes.
Retina	Layer of tissue on the back of the eye that contains the cells responsive to light (photoreceptors).
Rods	Photoreceptors in the retina that are most active in low light conditions.
Sclera	Protective coating around the back of the eyeball.
Vitreous humor	Clear, jelly-like fluid found in the back portion of the eye. Helps maintain the eye's shape.

Information for the Student: An Investigation of the Composition of Sunlight and Human Vision

In this unit, you will be studying the nature of light and human vision. You will perform several experiments and activities to learn more about this subject. Use the data you collect from your experiments to add information to your K-W-L charts.

The information and questions contained in your K-W-L charts will then serve as a starting point for an independent research project.

You will also conduct an ongoing survey of the media for examples of how optics and other light-related issues are portrayed.

To succeed in these activities, you will need to do research using a variety of media and information sources. As you perform your research, keep in mind the following questions:

- Where are the best places to find the information I need? What types of materials will be the most useful?

- Is the source for my information reliable and accurate? Who is providing the information?

- Is the information relevant? How does this source help me answer the questions I am being asked or solve the problem I am being posed?

- How can I organize the information I find to make effective use of it when I need it?

At the end of this unit, you will need to prepare a bibliography of the sources you used to find the information you need. A bibliography is a summary of the documents you used. The materials are described using a standard format so that other people can find the same information you did and conduct their own research into the topic.

As you work, make sure you record the following information about your sources. You should record:

1. The title of the book, article, video, or Web page you used;

2. The complete name of the author;

3. The publisher of the book or article, the producer of the video, or the website address;

4. The date of publication or the date the material was produced; and

5. The city in which the material was produced or published.

Collecting this information as you do your research will save you a great deal of time later. It will also help you locate information again if you need to refer back to something.

Keep all of your work on this project—notes, worksheets, and reference information—together in a file folder or binder.

Student Worksheet 8-2

Name _____ Date _____

Parts of the Eye

The list below describes various parts of the eye. Study the list. Write the definitions for each term on the lines beside each one. Then draw and label a diagram of the eye on the back of this sheet.

Aqueous Humor _____

Choroid _____

Cones _____

Cornea _____

Iris _____

Lens _____

Optic Nerve _____

Pupil _____

Retina _____

Rods _____

Sclera _____

Vitreous Humor _____

You will need to use a reference document or documents to complete this activity. List the bibliographic data for your sources here:

_____

_____

_____

Add new information you learn from this activity to your K-W-L chart.

Student Worksheet 8-3

Name _____ **Date** _____

Heat versus Light Experiment

Heat and light are both forms of electromagnetic radiation. To find out more about both, do this experiment.

Materials:
    2 thermometers
    black construction paper
    white construction paper
    tape

Procedure:

1. Make a cover for one thermometer by taping the black construction paper around it. Close one end with tape so that the thermometer won't fall out.

2. Make an identical cover for the second thermometer using the white construction paper.

3. Take the covered thermometers outside. Place them in full sun.

4. Predict what you think will happen to each thermometer. Write your prediction here:

_____

5. Wait three minutes. Slide each thermometer out of its cover. Read the temperatures. Record the results of your experiment in your science journal or on the back of this sheet.

6. How do you think light and heat are related?

_____

7. Add the new information you learned from this experiment to your K-W-L chart.

Student Worksheet 8-4

Name _____ **Date** _____

Why Is the Sky Blue?

Do this experiment to explore the colors we see in the afternoon sky and at sunrise and sunset.

Materials:
- transparent, round bowl (glass or plastic)
- water
- milk
- eyedropper
- flashlight
- sheet of white paper

Procedure:

1. Fill the bowl with water.

2. Using the eyedropper, add several drops of milk to the water in the bowl. Mix. The water should now appear cloudy. The milk will simulate dust and dissolved gases in the atmosphere.

3. Darken the room slightly. Shine the flashlight into the bowl of water. Describe what you see:

    _____

4. Next, hold the sheet of white paper on one side of the bowl. Shine the flashlight *through* the bowl so that the beam falls on the paper. Describe what you see:

    _____

5. Use the back of this sheet or your science journal to write the scientific explanation for the results of this experiment. Use reference materials as needed. (Make sure to create a bibliography of your sources!) Draw diagrams as needed.

6. Add the new information you learned from this experiment to your K-W-L chart.

Student Worksheet 8-5

Name _____ Date _____

The Color of Sunlight

In this activity, you will test various colors of light. You will also explore how different objects' appearances change in different colors of light.

Materials needed (for each lab group):

4-in-1 Light Source (provided by your teacher)

Ray Optics Kit (provided by your teacher)

colored construction paper: red, yellow, green, and blue

any opaque object

Procedure:

1. Place the Light Source Box on a white sheet of paper. Adjust it so the three primary colors (red, green, and blue) are showing.

2. Predict what color will result when the red, green, and blue lights combine. Write your prediction in the first row of the data table below.

3. Place the convex lens so that it focuses the light rays into a single point or band. What color do they form? Record the result in the first row of your data table.

4. Next, you will use any opaque object to block the green rays. Predict the results. Record your prediction in row 2 of the data table. Now do the trial. What secondary color results? Record the information in your data table.

5. Repeat Step 4, blocking first the blue, then the red light. Record your predictions and results for each trial in the table.

Colors combined:	Predicted color result:	Actual color result:
Red + blue + green		
Red + blue		
Red + green		
Green + blue		

6. Following a similar procedure, shine white, green, blue, and red light in succession onto the sheet of red construction paper. What color is the sheet under each light?

7. Repeat for each of the remaining colors of construction paper.

8. On the back of this sheet, create a data table to record your predictions and results.

9. Based on your observations, describe any patterns in the appearance of colored objects when they are illuminated by colored light. _____

10. What colors is white light made up of? _____

11. Add the new information you learned from this experiment to your K-W-L chart.

Student Worksheet 8-6

Name _____ **Date** _____

Newton and the Blue Light

Sir Isaac Newton (1642–1727) was a scientist and mathematician. Although he is most famous for his experiments with motion, Newton also investigated light and color.

Before Newton, scientists believed that light and color were not related. He devised a way to prove or disprove this idea.

In this activity, you will reproduce Newton's experiment.

Materials:
    white light source
    two prisms
    two opaque sheets of paper, such as black construction paper

Procedure:

1. Shine the light through one prism to create a "rainbow."

2. Fold each sheet of paper in half so that it can stand on its bent edge.

3. Place one sheet to the left of the "rainbow." Place the other to the right of the "rainbow."

4. Carefully adjust the positions of the papers so that they block all of the rays coming out of the prism *except* the blue ones.

5. You should now have a pure beam of blue light shining between the two opaque sheets of paper.

6. Place the second prism behind the first (on the far side of the paper barricades) so that the blue light shines through it.

7. Observe what comes through the other side of the second prism. Describe what you see here:

   _____

8. Go to a reference source to learn more about the history of this experiment. (Make sure to create a bibliography of your sources!) Compare Newton's findings with your own. On the back of this sheet or in your science journal, describe how this experiment proves the relationship between light and color.

9. Add the new information you learned from this experiment to your K-W-L chart.

Student Worksheet 8-7

Name _____ Date _____

Updating and Using Your K-W-L Chart
Research Project

Update your K-W-L chart. Study your W column. Choose a question or topic from this column that you would like to investigate further:

_____

Use at least **four** different sources to find out more about this subject. Make sure to keep a bibliography of your sources. Then write a short essay about this topic.

Your essay should include three main sections:

- An introductory paragraph,

- At least **five** body paragraphs, and

- A concluding paragraph.

Your *introductory paragraph* will set out the main purpose of your essay. You may need to perform your research before you can decide the main purpose.

Write one sentence that describes your main purpose here:

_____

_____

The *body* of your essay will provide the data that support your main point. Each category of data is given its own paragraph. The paragraph should also include details that illustrate the main idea of the paragraph.

List at least five categories of data that support your essay's main purpose. Each of these will become the foundation for its own paragraph.

Paragraph 1: _____

Paragraph 2: _____

Paragraph 3: _____

Paragraph 4: _____

Paragraph 5: _____

Additional paragraphs: _____

For each of the reasons you have listed above, be prepared to provide facts and other details to illustrate them. Use the space below to jot down your notes. If you cannot think of supportive details, you will have to go back to your original research notes or do additional research.

The *concluding paragraph* of your essay restates your main point. It also sums up the main ideas in each of your body paragraphs.

When you have completed your essay, make sure you proofread your work. Check for spelling and punctuation errors and factual accuracy. Revise your work as necessary.

Assessment for Written Presentation

Name _____ Date _____

Quality of Content

    3   Message is clear to the reader. All graphics support the presentation's main idea.

    2   The reader is unsure of the main message of the essay. Some graphics support the main idea. Others detract from the message.

    1   No clear message is presented. Graphics bear little relation to the main idea.

Organization

    3   Essay is well organized. Reader follows the presentation. Order of presentation makes sense. All essay elements—intro, body, conclusion—are present.

    2   Essay is somewhat organized. Most essay elements—intro, body, conclusion—are present. Essay is difficult to follow.

    1   Essay is not well organized. Most essay elements—intro, body, conclusion—are absent.

Style

    3   Essay is written with flair. Transitions between paragraphs and between types of material are handled smoothly. Graphics are attractively prepared and dynamically presented.

    2   Essay is competent. Transitions between paragraphs and between types of material are occasionally rocky. Graphics are adequate but not dynamic.

    1   Essay is workmanlike. Transitions between paragraphs and between types of materials are awkward and reveal a lack of preparation. Graphics are cursory and visually unexciting or completely absent.

Appearance

    3   Essay is exceptionally well presented. Spelling and grammar are correct. Graphics are aligned.

    2   Essay is neatly presented. Spelling and grammar are mostly correct. Graphics are mostly aligned and attractive.

    1   Essay is sloppy. Spelling and grammar show little accuracy and care. Graphics are messy or crooked.

Part 2—Using the Media to Explore Light, Optics, and Vision

Background Information for the Teacher and Library Media Specialist

In part 2 of this unit, students will conduct a study of three types of media to find examples of information that relate to the topic of light and vision. Students will keep a scrapbook of items collected from newspapers and magazines. They will maintain records of data collected from watching assorted television programs. Then they will evaluate various sources of information for accuracy and objectivity.

Lesson Outline

Explain to students that much of the information they receive comes from the media—newspapers, magazines, Internet, radio, and television. A large percentage of this information is aimed specifically at them. This is because students between the ages of 6 and 17 have enormous buying power. They spend over $100 billion (U.S.) of their own and their parents' money every year!

Ask students how they evaluate information they get from newspapers, TV, the Internet, etc. Where do they go for most of their information? How do they judge whether the information they are getting from this source is reliable?

Ask students which is more reliable, a journalist working for a newspaper or an advertisement. Why?

Explain to students why it is important to know their sources of information. For example, who is providing the information about a product or service, an event, or a person? What is their motivation? Is it being provided for profit, or as a public service? Is information from this source likely to be fair and unbiased, or slanted and unreliable?

Tell students that they will be conducting an independent investigation into media portrayals of optics and vision. They will create a scrapbook of clippings from their investigation. They will also analyze their findings and prepare answers to questions provided on handouts. At the end of the unit, students will hand in their scrapbooks for evaluation.

Student Worksheet 8-8

Name _____ Date _____

Using Media to Explore Light, Optics, and Vision

Much of the information that you get comes from the media—newspapers, magazines, Internet, radio, and television. Students your age are of great interest to the media. In fact, much of the media focuses on you. Why? Because you—young people between the ages of 6 and 17—spend over $100 billion (U.S.) of you own and your parents' money every year!

With all the media outlets and the products they sell clamoring for your dollars, it is important for you to *understand* the information they provide. For example, who is providing the information about a product or service, an event, or a person? What is their motivation? Is the information likely to be fair and unbiased, or slanted and unreliable?

In these five related activities, you will be using various media, including newspapers, magazines, and television, to find out more about light, optics, and vision. As you learn about these subjects, you will also learn to evaluate different sources of information for objectivity, veracity, and reliability.

At the end of the unit, you will hand in your scrapbook or science journal to your teacher for evaluation. Answer all of the questions on these worksheets before you hand in your work. Include your answers in your journal.

Materials:
    scrapbook or science journal
    scissors
    glue stick

Activity 1 Procedure:

1.   Using the **newspaper**, look for advertisements for the following products:

    • Scientific instruments such as microscopes or telescopes

    • Electronic equipment that use lenses or optical tools to work (e.g., DVD players, video recorders, optical scanners, or digital cameras)

2.   Cut out the articles and ads and glue them in your scrapbook. Then answer these questions:

    • How many *different* products did you find that rely on light and optics for their function?

    • What do the advertisements say about light, color, lenses, vision, or optics? Do they give any factual information?

Do you think scientific information about light, lenses, color, vision, or optics is necessary for people who are considering buying these products? Why or why not?

Who are these ads designed for?

Would you buy these products? Why or why not?

Activity 2 Procedure:

1. Look in the **newspaper** for articles or ads about kinds of eye surgery designed to improve vision.

2. Cut out the ads and glue them in your scrapbook. Then answer these questions:

   Which provided information that would be the most useful if you were deciding to undergo eye surgery, the ads or the articles? Why?

   Which pieces are presented in the most unbiased way? Would you trust this source for information?

   Make a list of the risks and benefits of one kind of eye surgery. Refer to advertisements for the surgery as well as to other sources, such as newspaper or magazine articles and Web sites. Would you undergo this surgery? Why or why not?

Activity 3 Procedure:

1. Photographs are important aspects of newspapers and magazines. Look in the **newspaper** and in **magazines** for examples of eye-catching photography.

2. Cut out the photographs and glue them in your scrapbook. Then answer these questions:

   • How do photographs change the way people read and understand newspapers and magazines?

   • How would newspapers and magazines be different if photographs were *not* used?

   • What makes a photograph eye-catching to you? How do you respond to black-and-white images versus color images?

   • When you turned the page of the magazine or newspaper, which did you look at first, pictures, text, or ads?

   • Can you tell if these photographs have been digitally altered? Do you think it matters if they have been? Do you think the media should be obligated to tell you if a photographic image has been altered? Why or why not?

Activity 4 Procedure:

You will need a clock with a second hand for this activity.

1. Choose two hours in which you can **watch television** undisturbed.

2. List each program and commercial that you watch during this time. List the start times, end times, and duration for each segment. Also indicate each time you change channels. Highlight what was on the screen at the time you changed the channel. Close your eyes periodically and just listen to the TV. Then answer these questions:

   • During each half-hour of television, how much time was devoted to commercials?

   • Compare a typical commercial to a typical television program, such as a drama or situation comedy. Which is louder? Which changes camera shots more often?

   • How many times did you see the same commercial during this viewing period? Why do you think advertisers repeat the same ad so many times during the same program, or on different channels at around the same time?

   • How important was *seeing* the action on the television compared to just listening to it? In what other ways is your sense of vision important?

Activity 5 Procedure:

1. Watch a national news broadcast on **television.** Count the number of news stories on the broadcast. Record how much time was devoted to each issue. Identify the major news story of the evening. How much time was devoted to this one story?

2. The next morning, read a national **newspaper.**

3. Cut out the articles related to this same news story. Glue them into your scrapbook. Then answer the following questions.

   • Which experience did you enjoy more, watching the news or reading the paper? Why?

   • How did the television presentation of the news differ from the newspaper coverage?

   • Which covered the story in greater depth, the TV or the newspaper?

   • How does seeing live video on TV differ from seeing a photograph in the newspaper?

   • From which do you think you will retain more information: the news broadcast or the newspaper articles? Why?

Assessment for Research Project

Name _____ **Date** _____

Assign 10 pts for each successfully completed component, for a possible score of 100.

(   ) Activity 1 Questions Clearly, Intelligently Answered

(   ) Activity 1 Clippings Present in Scrapbook; Selected Appropriately

(   ) Activity 2 Questions Clearly, Intelligently Answered

(   ) Activity 2 Clippings Present in Scrapbook; Selected Appropriately

(   ) Activity 3 Questions Clearly, Intelligently Answered

(   ) Activity 3 Clippings Present in Scrapbook; Selected Appropriately

(   ) Activity 4 Questions Clearly, Intelligently Answered

(   ) Activity 4 TV Viewing Record Present in Scrapbook

(   ) Activity 5 Questions Clearly, Intelligently Answered

(   ) Activity 5 Clippings Present in Scrapbook; Selected Appropriately

Organizational and Assessment Checklist for the Teacher

Lesson Component	Taught/Assessed by	Assessment Method
Introducing the Lesson —General Introduction • Identifying sources • How to prepare a bibliography • How to use a K-W-L chart		
Parts of the Eye		• Review Worksheet 8-2 answers for student comprehension of the material
Heat vs. Light Experiment • Supervise lab activity		• Review Worksheet 8-3 data and answers for student comprehension of the material • Review K-W-L chart
Why Is the Sky Blue? • Supervise lab activity		• Review Worksheet 8-4 data and answers for student comprehension of the material • Review K-W-L chart
The Color of Sunlight • Supervise lab activity		• Review Worksheet 8-5 data and answers for student comprehension of the material • Review K-W-L chart
Newton and the Blue Light • Supervise lab activity		• Review Worksheet 8-6 data and answers for student comprehension of the material • Review K-W-L chart
Updating and Using Your K-W-L Chart Research Project		• Review Worksheet 8-7 answers for student comprehension of the material • Assessment for Written Presentation
Introduction to Part 2		
Using Media to Explore Light Optics, and Vision Scrapbook Project Assign and supervise 5 sub-activities		Assessment for Research Project

Selected Suggested Resources/Bibliography

Items marked with an asterisk would be suitable for teacher background; all others would be for both teacher and student reference.

Laboratory Materials

The *4-in-1 Light Source* (Product #OS-8517A) and *Ray Optics Kit* (Product #OS-8516A) used in the color of light activity are available through PASCO Scientific Inc., 10101 Foothills Blvd., Roseville, CA 95747 (www.pasco.com, 800-772-8700, 916-786-3800). Other materials for the study of light, such as prisms and lenses, are also available through this source.

Web Sites

http://micro.magnet.fsu.edu/primer/lightandcolor/primaryhome.html
 This comprehensive, educational Web site covers all areas of optics and vision, including microscopy. Lots of activities and teacher resources. Highly recommended.

http://faculty.washington.edu/chudler/bigeye.html
 Solid information about eye anatomy and structure.

*School.discovery.com/lessonplans/programs/eye/
 Activities for middle school include projects, background information.

Users.rcn.com/jkimball.ma.ultranet/ BiologyPages/V/Vision.html
 Solid, more advanced information about eye anatomy.

www.physicsclassroom.com/Class/refrn/U14L6a.html
 Complete lesson on the human eye.

http://dibinst.mit.edu/BURNDY/Collections/Babson/OnlineNewton/Opticks.htm
 Online edition of *Opticks*, in which Newton's experiments with light are described.

http://www.timelinescience.org/resource/students/newton/light.htmhttp://www.visionscience.com/
 Historical and biographical information on Newton.

http://www.phy.hr/~dpaar/fizicari/xnewton.html
 Historical and biographical information on Newton.

www.kie.berkeley.edu/ned/data/E01-961012-004/full.html
 History, diagrams, and photographs showing Newton's blue light experiment.

http://www.yorku.ca/eye/thejoy.htm
 Comprehensive overview of science of vision.

http://www.discoveryfund.org/anatomyoftheeye.html
 Thorough discussion of eye anatomy.

http://webexhibits.org/causesofcolor/index.html
 Excellent exploration of color perception.

http://www.ebiomedia.com/gall/eyes/nocturnal.html
 Site examining animal night vision.

http://cvs.anu.edu.au/andy/beye/beyehome.html
   Includes nifty simulation of how honeybees see.

http://www.sbnp.org/Wetlands/text/00-7-2-4.htm
   Surveys structure of a wide variety of animal eyes.

www.pasco.com
   Science school supplier; also offers educational activities and links.

Print Resources

Burnie, D. *Light (The Eyewitness Science Series, 2)*. New York: DK Publishing, 1992.

Ditchburn, R. *Light*. Mineola, NY: Dover Publications, 1991.

*Hecht, E. "The Propagation of Light." In *Optics*, 4th ed., 86–148. San Francisco: Addison-Wesley, 2002.

*Kuehni, R. *Color: An Introduction to Practice and Principles*. New York: Wiley, 1997.

Maiklem, L., and W. Lach, eds. *Ultimate Visual Dictionary of Science*. New York: DK Publishing, 1998.

*Ronchi, V. *Optics, the Science of Vision*. Mineola, NY: Dover Publications, 1991.

Wade, N. *A Natural History of Vision*. Cambridge, MA: MIT Press, 1998.

Index

About the Author

HELAINE BECKER is an experienced educational writer currently living in Toronto, specializing in math, science, and language arts, with over 90 published works. She has written science materials for American Educational Products and J. Weston Walch, spelling supplementals for Rigby, middle school level biographies for school library publisher Blackbirch Press, and math and language materials for Learning Resources.

CLARK LANE MIDDLE SCHOOL
LIBRARY MEDIA CENTER
WATERFORD, CT 06385

DATE DUE

Demco